I0388698

Crash Test Parents

Parenthood: Has Anyone Seen My Sanity?

Other books in the Crash Test Parents series:

*Crash Test Parents Guide to Surviving a Year**
*Crash Test Parents Guide to Self-Esteem**

*Available only at www.racheltoalson.com/freebook

To see all the books Rachel has written, please click or visit the link below:
www.racheltoalson.com/store

Rachel Toalson

Parenthood: Has Anyone Seen My Sanity?

BATLEE PRESS

Batlee Press
PO Box 591596
San Antonio, TX 78259

The author appreciates your taking the time to read her work. Please consider leaving a review wherever you bought it, or telling your friends how much you enjoyed it. Both of those help spread the word, which is incredibly important for authors. Thank you for your support.
www.racheltoalson.com
www.crashtestparents.com

Manufactured in the United States of America

First Edition—2017/Cover designed by Toalson Marketing
www.toalsonmarketing.com

To all parents, everywhere, who are at their wits' end

R.T.

Contents

Foreword

Parents today are so busy they can hardly even remember what their name is (besides Mom and Dad). I know. I have six wild little boys climbing all over me, begging me for a snack, as I type out this letter to you right now. "In a minute," I say, which makes it even worse, because then they're whine-begging.

In a season like this, it can feel nearly impossible to do practically anything for yourself—especially read. So I'm very, very grateful that you have picked up this book at all. I now want to assure you that I wrote this book with you, busy parent, in mind. The chapters are broken down into easily consumable sections. Each section is a short essay on one aspect of parenting—such as leaving the house with kids, teaching kids autonomy, well meant parenting advice that's bogus after the first kid. You can read one little section at a time as you have a minute or two, or, if you're feeling adventurous, read it all in one sitting. I must warn you, though, that kids, if you haven't already noticed, have an amazing ability to tell when a parent is not paying attention. Once, when I was trying to finish a book I couldn't put down, my 6-year-old inhaled two pounds of carrots and had explosive diarrhea for the rest of the day. Also, my twins found a secret permanent marker stash and colored their faces green and purple. And my oldest, in typical idealist fashion, took down every book from our shelves that he planned to read in the next thirty-five years and then conveniently forgot how to put them back.

If your kids are sleeping, go ahead and settle in. If they're not, take it one section at a time.

I feel it must also be said that the essays in this book are not intended to prescribe a particular way of parenting. This book is a humor book, which means I'm mostly making fun of myself and my family and our interactions with one another. I believe other parents deal with some of the same issues that crop up in my home, but I do not have answers to every question. I only have humorous tries. Sometimes my kids do really shocking things, as I'm sure most kids do. Sometimes I have absolutely no idea how to get through a ridiculously difficult moment. Those moments, however, make for good humor essays in hindsight, which makes me glad I went through every twist and turn on the obstacle course called Parenthood.

I hope that in the pages to come, you will feel not only entertained but also empowered. I hope that you will know, in the deepest places one can know, that you are not the only not-perfect parent out there (I know it can seem like we're in the minority. There are more of us than we think). Parenting is hard sometimes (not all the time). Parenting is wonderful sometimes (not all the time.)

So wherever you find yourself as you pick up this book, know that you are a good parent, you can do this, and laughter really is the best medicine.

Coming to Terms with Your New Parent Reality

Things You Don't Consider Before Becoming a Parent

Whether or not you want to become a parent is relatively easy to decide. Those tiny little babies. So cute. So cuddly. So snuggly and soft and warm. Smelling of…

Well, everything nice, of course.

So when it came time for Husband and me to discuss the possibility of starting a family, it wasn't such a hard decision. I wanted one of those tiny cute cuddly babies. It was time.

What you don't consider before you decide to have a baby is that one day that baby will be a willful 3-year-old. And then he'll be a spirited 8-year-old. And then she'll be, God help you, 13.

It's not just the emotional and physical expenditure that will change as your tiny little baby, who only wants to eat and sleep and poop and stays put wherever you lay him, grows. Your entire lifestyle will change. We weren't ready for this. I don't know if any parent is, because these are the things you don't think about—and no one tells you—when all you can see is BABY.

I think about them now. Every time I get a utility bill in the mail or shop for groceries or just try to do something as simple as leaving the house.

What you don't think about is that when your baby becomes a kid, there's

The much higher utility bills.

You won't notice this one right away, because, well, babies stay put. They don't know how to turn on lights, which is your saving grace for a couple of years. You won't run into this problem until your kid gets really good at turning on lights but doesn't as quickly figure out how to turn them off. Or ever figure it out, which is more likely the case. You'll leave the house following behind Kid 1 while Kid 2 follows behind you, looking for something. And everyone knows that to look for something, you need lights.

Someday, when the baby is no longer a baby, he will also enjoy plugging up a toilet with toilet paper so he has to flush five times in a row and the toilet never fills up so it runs for half an hour before you notice. He'll forget to completely turn off the bathroom faucet after he's finally, finally, finally brushed his teeth after your thirtieth time asking, and it will run all night, because you were too worn out to stumble out of your bed, again, to check. He'll one day be 3 and think it's funny to see your face turn purple when he sneaks into the backyard and lets the water hose run, and the only way you know is when you're going out to put the trash in the bin and you slip in a gigantic mud puddle and call Husband home because a sprinkler has busted and you don't know what to do (Nope. It's just the 3-year-old, watering the grass. For five hours).

Higher utility bills. There's not much you can do about them, unless you cancel all your utilities and Little House on the Prairie it.

The grocery bill that will make you weep.

It doesn't matter if you're breastfeeding or bottle feeding, you are in for a treat. You won't even recognize your grocery budget in a few years. Kids are always, always, always hungry, always, and you certainly don't want them bumming food off their friends at school, because you know what happens when they get sugar in their system. (What happens? Read on.)

The fact that bouncing off the walls is a real thing.

You will watch them do it after attending their friend's birthday parties. You'll see the evidence in wall nicks and holes their hands accidentally made in doors when they ran into it too hard, and you'll make a mental note to fix them all, but it will never happen. Because kids. And then you will vow never, ever to let them go to another birthday party. Ever. And then another invitation will come three days later, because they're in kindergarten and all twenty-five students have birthdays, and they have to invite everyone in their class, because this is the school rule. Kids' self esteem is precious, you see.

And, because he got an invitation and he sometimes talks to the girl in class, you will, in the end, let him go to another birthday party, thus beginning the cycle all over again.

The gross, gross and grosser.

You will do grosser things than you ever thought you'd do. Ever. Because sometimes there will be a little boy who took his favorite Lightning McQueen car to the potty with him, because Lightning "wanted to watch," and now Lightning is sitting in the toilet your boy just went #2 in, and you will have to reach your hand into that stank and pull Lightning back out. Getting a new one just won't do. Plus, remember the higher utility bills? Yeah, that goes for clogged pipes, too. Close your eyes and fish it out. There's soap for that. Lots and lots of soap.

You may also be sitting enjoying a lovely dinner with friends when your 18-month-old starts upchucking something that looks like a cross between a cauliflower smoothie and no-butter mashed potatoes, and, rather than let it fall on the floor and make someone else clean it up with their handy mop and bucket, your reflexes will make you catch it. In your hands. Your bare hands. Your bare hands that just stuck a fry in your mouth. (You'll never see those "friends" again, by the way. They don't have kids. They don't understand.)

And you may quite possibly open a door to a poop explosion every other day if you have twins who think it's funny to take their diapers off and time their bowel movements for the exact moment they're supposed to be sleeping for naps, and you will have to scrub it off all the cracks they've made in their cribs. Don't worry. There's soap for that, too.

The energy it takes to keep a house tidy.

It's not even worth it. They'll just undo all your work anyway. Hang up their winter jacket on the peg where it goes? In five minutes they'll decide they want to wear it in the "fall-ish" weather that blew in, bringing temperatures from 125 to 115 degrees. Get their school papers all organized and nice? They'll want to show you something they made in school today, and it'll all end up on the floor anyway. Have a place for their shoes? Doesn't matter. They won't end up there. Save your energy for others things. Like putting them back in bed four hundred times.

The paradoxical emotions.

There is the one minute where you feel angry enough to strangle your 3-year-old because, for the four billionth time, he marked in a library book while you were watching, just to do it, and then there's the moment (after ten minutes of cool down and maybe a ~~bottle~~ glass of wine) when he brings you the library book and asks you to read to him, and his eyes are so dang beautiful, and yes, of course you'll do this for your precious little baby. There's the second where you want to lock them out of your room forever and ever and ever because they keep coming in to ask questions like "Do penguins have knees" and "Why can't we have four dogs" and "How did I get out of your body when I was a baby," and all you know is you want to go to sleep, and then there is that other second where he comes in one more time and you take a deep breath and all he wants is another kiss and hug you don't often get anymore because he's getting too big too fast.

There's the moment when you can't stand the sight of him because he just ate his brother's vitamins he knows he's not supposed to touch (you've done this dance half a million times), and then there's the other moment when you can't stand how much you love him.

You'll get used to these moments as a parent.

The torturous road trips.

Soon, going anywhere outside a ten-mile radius of your home will feel like torture. This is mostly because of the question, "Are we almost there?" which will come out of their mouths exactly five minutes after packing in the car. And since you haven't even left the driveway, you'll know it's going to be a really long trip. This question will be asked every other minute for as long as it takes to get you anywhere. So just keep the travel short, if you know what's best for you. And if this question doesn't bother you so much, there will be other things. I Spy, for example. And Disney songs. And farts in an enclosed space.

The impossible: Leaving the house.

You're all dressed and put together and ready to go? All of you at the same time? Well, congratulations, because someone's about to puke all over himself. You made it out to the car and everyone's strapped? Someone will say his shoes aren't actually in the van like he thought, and could you help him find a pair, and you'll spend the next forty-five minutes looking for the matches to five lone shoes. You're about to walk out the door on time for once? Someone will discover how to open their Thermos of milk and dump it all over their brother's backside.

Late just comes with being a parent. Don't let anyone tell you any different, and don't let anyone make you feel guilty about it, either. They have no idea what it's like to leave with neanderthals in tow.

That feeling you get.

No, I'm not talking about the anger or the frustration or the fear that maybe we shouldn't have done what we did. I mean the overwhelming emotion that hits us every time they're doing something amazing or wonderful or they say something brilliant or funny or they're just sitting there doing nothing. It's that feeling of love that launches us through all these unforeseen challenges.

So I guess if I'm weighing the options, I'd have to say that The Feeling outweighs all the rest.

But ask me again in a eight years, when my grocery bill is like a second and third mortgage because I'll be living with ~~a swarm of locusts~~ five teenagers.

What I Never Expected From a Household of Boys

When I began my parenting journey, I did not realize I would have six children. Three was the "reasonable" number we'd decided on when Husband and I had that first conversation about our married futures and what our family might look like someday.

I don't really know what happened. We changed our minds. We were surprised (at least by the extra twin). We were...a little crazy, maybe?

I didn't expect so many children to call me Mama. But what I really didn't expect was for all of them to be boys.

When the sonogram proved the first one was a boy, I remember thinking, "I don't even know what to do with boys. I won't be able to fix their hair or play with dolls or read girly stories like *Anne of Green Gables* or *The Little Princess* or *Little House on the Prairie.*" I, once the official French braider for my high school volleyball team, was good at that stuff.

I remember thinking, "I don't know if I'll be any good at boys."

Now, eight years later, with six of them destroying my house on a minute-by-minute basis, I have no idea what I would even do with a girl. Even still, there are some elusive mysteries about this so-different gender that confound me to this day.

I thought I might celebrate my boys by sharing some. (Note: Some of them might be cross-gender, but I just wouldn't know.)

Stripping off clothes as soon as they walk through the door.

They're not allowed outside without clothes or only in their underwear, but that's OK. They'll just play inside in their underwear, or with nothing on at all, even though it's a perfect afternoon for riding scooters or swinging or running laps around the cul-de-sac. They want to be where they can wear the fewest clothes, and since that's inside, well, here they are.

Leaving stripped clothes on the floor. No matter how many times I remind them where the laundry hamper is, my living room floor is like a playground for errant socks and dirty shirts. Even though the shoes have an easy, designated place, they hardly ever make it there. Even though my boys know perfectly well how to hang shirts and fold shorts, they'll likely skip this step in favor of something easier—like a shirt-carpet, perhaps. Even though the hamper is two inches from where they dropped their discarded clothes, they will not even notice.

Shoes worn out three weeks after I bought them. They run too fast or kick poles with friends at recess or use their toes as a scooter brake (Hey boys: there's a perfectly efficient one attached to the back of your scooter).

Hysterical laughter anytime someone farts or pretends to. It never, ever, ever gets old. To them.

Pride in owning up to the fart, especially if it's smelly. Even the 2-year-old twins are now saying "I tooted" (we don't allow the use of the word "fart" until a boy is 10 years old. You know, rites of passage and such.) and grinning about it. Apparently this is something to be immensely proud of in the world of boy. And the more people you can knock out with your flappy-cheeked vibrations, the better.

Everything is a competition. Running down the stairs. Setting the table. Talking.

So.much.noise. We had to buy a megaphone just to be heard over the constant noise, because we were damaging our vocal chords trying to yell instructions over the six competing voices that are somehow twenty times louder than ours.

Death-defying acts. Like jumping from the ninth stair onto the bottom floor of our house. Like swinging as high as they can possibly swing and then jumping from the height to see if they'll land on their feet. Like hanging upside down from monkey bars I can't even reach from the ground, while I stand "spotting" them, unsure of what I'll do if their legs slip and they come bowling toward me.

Story times that don't look like your average story times. Stories are important in our house, but if you were to take a peek inside our home library any evening at 7:15, you would see quite a spectacle, because boys are standing on their heads and sitting on a tower of pillows, trying not to fall, and practicing their break-dance moves in the middle of the floor. But they're listening, somehow. I know. I've tested them to be sure.

Total obsession with their boy-parts. "Stop playing with your penis." I say this several times a day.

Everything becomes a weapon. An empty paper towel roll, dug out of the recycling basket = a sword. A PVC pipe that's supposed to be holding up the soccer net out back = a bazooka (they don't even know what that is. They just shoot.). A scooter = a machine for smashing slower brothers' toes.

Wet dog smell when they come back in from playing outside,

even if it's 40 degrees out there.

Bath time where soap misses the hair and face, even though I'm right there to remind them. "I don't care if I smell," they say. Well, okay then. At least it'll keep the girls away for now.

No underwear in their drawers three days after I've done laundry because they spent a week playing Captain Underpants and actually, for once, put all the underpants worn on their head in the laundry basket.

Nakedness. All the time. Everywhere. Company's over? No matter. They'll come out of the bathroom anyway. Immediately after bath time, it takes at least five reminders for each of them to even locate their pajamas (in the same drawer they're always in) and five more for them to actually put them on. I'm pretty sure this is just a twenty-minute stalling technique meticulously planned to get them more naked time.

This is not an exhaustive list of all their wild and crazy, by any means.

But with all the nose-wrinkling smells and the heart-stopping tricks and the mess that follows them like Charlie Brown's "Pig Pen," there sure is a lot of love for their mama.

They love like little hurricanes, pulling up the roots of scars I've carried my whole life, smashing windows and walls so I'm brave enough to bare the very heart of me, tearing off a roof and twisting me toward a height I could never imagine.

I did not expect this, either.

What these years with boys have shown me is that I am a woman beloved times six.

And I wouldn't trade that for an impeccably tidy house that

smells nice all the time or a heart that beats calm or children who sit perfectly still and quiet and calm at a word or look from me.

I wouldn't trade it for all the riches in the world, because I already have those riches, climbing across tables to get more food and hanging from ceiling fans when they think I'm not looking and flipping off beds when they should be sleeping.

Riches beyond compare.

Sleep While the Baby Sleeps and Other Unhelpful Advice

They say sleep deprivation is a lot like walking around drunk.

That must be why I keep running into doors and passing out on the couch and forgetting where in the world I put the new baby's clean diaper when it's literally right in front of my face—I'm looking at it and it's looking at me and I STILL can't see it.

After the first baby, all those people who have walked in our shoes give us that helpful advice: "Sleep when the baby sleeps." And if you're like me, you don't realize they're serious until you've spent sixty hours awake.

People also give this advice after baby number two and baby number three, which always makes me wonder if they ever really had more than one. It's just not helpful advice once you've passed the first baby.

Kids, you see, at least a tribal group like mine, need constant supervision. The only time I sleep is when they're ALL sleeping. Which is never.

(Actually that's not true. My kids sleep like champs. In their beds by 8:30, the first one usually falls asleep by 8:45, and the last one by 10, and then that first one will wake up by 6. Which leaves me a whole four hours for sleep, after I finally wind down from the thirteen times I almost dropped into dreamland only to hear a knock on my door from the one who needs to tell me about that new character he's developing for the story he's writing or another one who needs to tattle on a brother for kicking him in the face or another who just wants his third kiss goodnight.)

Sleep while the baby sleeps.

Oh, I wish it were that easy.

Once, when I slept while the baby was sleeping, my 8-year-old, 5-year-old and 4-year-old boys climbed to the top of our minivan parked out front and decided to see what it would be like to pee off the top, in clear view of every house on the block (sorry neighbors). Another time I passed out involuntarily, I woke with a start, five minutes later, because I heard something clinking in the background. Turns out it was my 2-year-old twins, racing out the back door with knives they wanted to use for sword fighting. And how could I possibly forget the time I took a twelve-second nap and my 5-year-old ate two pounds of grapes?

Sleep while the baby sleeps.

It's just not helpful anymore.

Another piece of used-to-be-helpful advice that is no longer relevant after the first child: **Take care of yourself.**

Well, see, I tried it one time. I tried putting up my feet for ten minutes of quiet in my bedroom. Just ten minutes. When I came back out there were one hundred paper airplanes scattered all over our living room floor. Another time I went to the bathroom for no more than two minutes, and my third son located a black permanent marker and turned his yellow shirt into a black-and-yellow striped shirt. Impressive, but that doesn't come out. And then there was that time I felt brave enough to rinse off in a fifty-two-second shower, and my 5-year-old used the time to cut a chunk out of his hair, draw whiskers on his face and glue his hand to his shirt.

"Hold him all you can. It sure goes fast," they say.

Yes. I know. This isn't my first infant. That's part of the problem.

I tried holding him every minute I could. And then a 2-year-old figured out how to open the under-sink cabinets, even though they're baby proofed, and sprayed vinegar cleaner all over the floor so his twin brother would slip in it, flip his feet over his face, and bust his head on the tile floor. There was that time at the children's museum I tried to hold him and stare in his eyes for five seconds or so, and the 2-year-olds snuck into an elevator and we searched for them for twenty whole minutes, nearly giving them up for lost before the elevator door dinged and out they came running with grins on their faces and not enough vocabulary to tell us what exactly they were doing in there.

Once, when I thought I'd feed the baby in the privacy of my room so we could share some one-on-one time, because the 2-year-olds were sleeping, one woke up, unbeknownst to me, and colored his entire door red. It's still a mystery how that happened, since their room holds NOTHING but beds and clothes. I think he was hiding it under his tongue.

OK, kids. You win.

I just can't use all that well-meant advice anymore.

When I was talking it over with Husband, trying to figure out a new plan, some way we might be able to sleep while the baby was sleeping and hold him all we could and actually take care of ourselves, he looked at me for a minute and said, "Maybe we just need to buy some kennels."

I think he might be on to something.

No, I'm Not Still Pregnant. This is Just My After-Belly.

It was date night, the first one since having our new baby twelve days before. We'd just finished our dinner and decided to stop by the store to pick up a few baby necessities, since our son was sleeping soundly in his car seat (which we carried into the store, don't worry. I'm not a completely incompetent parent.) and the other five were at home (hopefully) asleep with a sitter.

We were almost through the checkout line when a woman rolled into the space behind us. She had her grandbaby sitting in the basket, chattering in an unknown baby language. Her husband stood behind her.

And because I'd just pulled up the car seat cover to check on my little one, she noticed him and said, "Oh my goodness! You have a brand new baby!"

"Yes, ma'am," I said politely as Husband stood paying. I turned to put the bags in the cart.

That's when her husband said, "Oh, looks like she's got another one on the way!" all excited and proud of himself for noticing.

And I swear we heard that woman say, "Uh-oh," while Husband and I tried to hold it together. We made it all the way to the exit doors before we burst out laughing. We laughed all the way home.

The next day, thirteen days postpartum, we stopped to get an oil change at this place Husband frequents, where you can just sit in the car while they do a quick change. No kids need to be unbuckled or entertained or chased away from the parking lot. It's the best idea ever. There should be more places like this.

The attendant knew Husband, but I'd never met him before. Still, when we were leaving, he assumed familiarity, calling, "See you soon, man," to Husband and then flippantly remarking, "Not you, I guess. I'll see you after."

Husband quickly rolled up the window, and I tried not to laugh while in clear view, until Husband said what I was thinking. "After what?"

Some men are just clueless.

But lest we go easy on females and chalk it up to men not knowing any better, I must tell you the story of a woman we met at a park one week after I gave birth to twins.

Our twins, who collectively weighed ten pounds at the time of delivery, were born six weeks early, so we had to leave them in neonatal intensive care for a while, but because our other boys weren't allowed in the NICU unit and one of their birthdays was coming up, we decided one day to take them to the park and visit the twins later that evening.

They were playing like children do, making friends with another little boy, and his mother ambled over. We got to talking about how I only have boys, and it wasn't long before she gestured toward my postpartum belly and said, "Is this one a girl?"

"Oh, no," I said, laughing, because I knew this was about to get awkward. I really didn't blame her. My uterus had a lot of shrinking to do after twins. So I kept it nice and gentle. "No, I just had twin boys six days ago. They're in the NICU right now."

She nodded and said, "Oh," like she understood, but clearly she didn't, because her next words were, "So when are they due?"

I had to explain it all over again, and she apologized profusely and then gathered up her son and hightailed it out of there.

I didn't mean to make her uncomfortable. But such is life when we're looking through the lens of assumptions.

Nine years ago, when my first baby was born and those eating disorders and body image issues still stood way too close, these experiences would have really bothered me, but today I know the truth of it. I know that something incredibly amazing happens to a woman's body when she's growing a human being. I know that in the days after, her stomach won't just POOF! back into place.

You see, the uterus has fed and housed a new baby for nine whole months, and it can't be rushed in its shrinking back to normal. Shrinking takes time. It's not done in a day or a week or even three. For a time, we will still look just a little bit pregnant, with a bump that could go either way. (And it's different for every woman, so comparisons aren't constructive.)

So when is it okay to assume that a woman is pregnant?

Never.

But if you really want to try (God help you), and you're feeling brave, here are some (mostly) foolproof giveaways:

1. She doesn't have a newborn baby with her.
2. She tells you she's expecting.
3. She doesn't say she just had a baby.
4. She announced a pregnancy on social media but she hasn't yet announced a birth.

If you've checked all the above and answered no, there's one really important one left:

5. Her stomach looks like it's housing an oversized basketball, she's almost doing a standing backbend and she's waddling significantly. And I mean *significantly*, because yesterday was her due date.

That's it. Any other time? Just keep your mouth shut.

Better safe than sorry.

I Used to Want to Be a Rockstar. This is All I Got.

Husband and I used to be in a band. Well, we still are. We just don't ever play the songs we're still writing, because we have six kids. But before those six kids, we played all over Texas and took a few tours through Arizona, Colorado, and New Mexico. We wrote our own songs and practiced every day and stayed up way too late playing gigs.

When the first son was born, we continued our pursuit, because we enjoyed doing it and wanted, secretly, to be rockstars. And Son #1 was super easy to pack up and take along with us, because he loved music and enjoyed meeting new people who fawned all over him and was amazingly tolerant of long trips.

Son #2 came along two years later, and it was still relatively easy. We just packed for two kids instead of one. We brought a friend along who could watch the kids while we did our hour-long set on stage, and then I'd rescue the friend while Husband and the other band members went to talk to people at the merch table.

Then came Son #3. I won't say he meant to change everything. It's just the logistics of it. When parents go from two to three kids, everything gets real. You've suddenly run out of hands. And eyes. And ability to focus.

Two weeks after he was born, we boarded a plane to fly to Arizona and record our third album, and we took them all with us so I could worry the whole time about what if the oldest wandered off when one of us wasn't looking because the baby needed to be fed and he was still so tiny and cute and wonderful and I just couldn't take my eyes off him but I also couldn't take my eyes off the older walking ones. We made it, with twelve new gray hairs that I hide well beneath strategic combing.

But when it came time to promote our album, here's where the "we can still do this" really fell through. Because there aren't a whole lot of people who enjoy watching a 3-year-old, a 16-month-old and a one-month-old. We tried to limp along for a while, and then the twins came along and life was completely over. Because twins.

Ever since I was a little kid I've wanted to be two things: a writer and a rock star. I get to be one of them, writing every single day of my life, and it's bliss. And, for the other, well, this is all I got.

Being a rockstar used to mean fame.

I know it sounds shallow to put it like that, but doesn't any performer who's good at what they do dream of this? Packed crowds chanting the band's name and singing along to songs with their camera phones as "lighters?" Fans wanting to meet us just to shake our hand or say a few words to us? People dancing in their places or moshing or whatever kids do these days, even if they can't hear a note of the music because they're screaming too loudly?

Actually, this sounds exactly like my house. There's a packed crowd chanting my name when it's time for dinner and I haven't started anything yet. There's a line of kids wanting a minute of our attention because they have to tell us their brother took the toy they were playing with and they're really sad about that and they need help getting it back. And there are little boys dancing or moshing (mostly unintentionally, but this is what happens when you're eight people in a small living room and Imagine Dragons is playing on Pandora) and screaming so loudly you can't hear a note of the music because we're playing one of the songs we wrote for them and they just want "If You're Happy and You Know It" or the Kidz Bop version of anything Taylor Swift.

Being a rockstar used to mean wealth.

Another shallow one, I know. But we had dreams, you see. We would make the big bucks with *just our music.* Who gets to make the big bucks doing what they love? And we would use those big bucks to build schools for orphaned children and dig wells for the people who don't have access to clean water, and after all that, we'd use the leftover funds for dinners out when we didn't feel like cooking and a house with as many rooms as we needed and expensive parties.

I guess this one looks like my life today, too, because when I don't feel like cooking there's always a picnic dinner out at the park that we'll pack ourselves (but it's still not cooking!) and a house with...enough rooms and birthday parties at home with twenty 6-year-olds running wild on cake and cookies and lavender tea that's supposed to balance those effects but clearly doesn't.

Being a rockstar used to mean writing original songs.

We used to dream of writing a new song every week and sharing it with the world. We used to dream of changing lives with our melodies. We used to dream of hearing those songs on the radio and imagining others singing along.

We still write original songs. It's just that they're mostly about farts and poop and cleaning too much earwax out of an ear. Everything a boy thinks is hilarious, but at least we've got our adoring (or laughing) fans.

Being a rockstar used to mean practicing a whole song without a kid interruption.

We used to be able to practice for two hours, uninterrupted, song after song after song, and this made us really, really good. We could take our time and run the parts that gave us trouble last week and perfect every song before we shared it with the world.

And I guess if you're getting all technical we can still practice a song, or thirty seconds of it, give or take a few, without a kid interruption, and you do get really good at accommodating this sort of thing when you have kids. Husband and I can keep a conversation going for an entire day, even with ten thousand five-minute interruptions. We can even maintain it when the interruptions are things like "Why is my poop lime green?" and "What happens when a bird crashes into the window, because one just did?" and "I just answered the door and one of the twins ran out with a man I've never seen before." It's quite a skill. So thanks, kids, for that valuable gift.

Being a rockstar used to mean a whole crew of roadies.

Roadies are people who carry all the heavy stuff and help set up the equipment and wait around until the show is over just so they can help you do it all again. They're pretty handy people.

And I suppose, in a way, I still have roadies, because when we go to the local museum, the 8-year-old does do the heavy lifting with those books he likes to bring everywhere, even though we didn't ask him to bring them. And the 5-year-old will load up that backpack with a thousand stuffed animals he wanted to bring along so they could see the lions at the zoo, and he'll carry it the whole time. And one of the 3-year-olds will always try to get the picnic lunch out of the car and accidentally dump it out on the sidewalk so the birds come swooping. I know. He's just trying to help, like roadies do.

Being a rockstar used to mean a whole closet of cool clothes.

I thought long and hard about what I wanted to look like on stage. I was the only female in a band of males, and I needed to stand out. Be noticed. That meant bold colors and dramatic makeup and shoes that were comfortable but still said "Woman."

And it's true that I do wear a bright orange workout shirt about once a week with my uniform workout pants, and I have gone dramatic with the makeup and adopted the "naked face" look, and my shoes do say "Woman" because they're fluorescent pink running shoes that allow me to chase after my 3-year-olds when they get a wild hair every other minute and decide they're going to sprint in two different directions and see who Mama catches first. My cool clothes have just become be-prepared-to-run-at-all-times clothes.

Being a rockstar used to mean a glamorous life.

Of course we would meet all the famous people, like Simon Cowell or Ed Sheeran or maybe just Adam Sandler. We'd sit down to fancy dinners and wipe our mouths with silky napkins and engage in stimulating conversation. We would get in the car and cruise to a party at any hour of any day.

Okay, so, yes, I get to meet famous people like the 8-year-old's principal or the 5-year-old's best friend (he talks about her ALL THE TIME) and I get to sit down to a dinner of sun-roasted tomato parmesan pasta with the cloth napkins we made ourselves and engage in stimulating conversation about how we could do a sugar experiment with ice cream and root beer, because that's what they did in class today and they DRANK IT ALL AND IT WAS SO

YUMMY and now they can't stay at the table because they have too much energy and they need to ruuuuuuunnnn. And even though it takes us three hours just to leave the house, we still get to go to the occasional party when the kids are invited (sitters for six kids are hard to find). What kind of person would want to party at all hours of the day, anyway? My kids are up all hours of the day. Midnight and I have become intimately familiar, and let me just tell you, he's pretty exhausting.

I used to want to be a rockstar. And this is all I got.

But you know what? I don't think this parenting gig was the short end of the stick at all. Mostly because I get to feel like a rockstar every single day. I feel like a rockstar when my kid is whining and I just can't take it anymore and I miraculously don't yell but calmly say that his whining makes me feel like the tea kettle that's going off on the stove. I feel like a rockstar when I finally get dinner on the table without losing my mind from all the "I'm hungrys" following me around and not one of them complains about what we're having for once. I feel like a rockstar every time I get out the door in the morning with all six kids dressed and wearing mostly matching shoes.

I feel like a rockstar when I climb out of bed after a night cleaning up puke. I feel like a rockstar when I remember my toothbrush on a trip, because I usually pack for the kids first. I feel like a rockstar when they smile at me after a long day like I'm the most important person in the world to them.

Every parent who is raising a human being to be a decent person is a rockstar, because we have legions of adoring fans (okay, a handful at the most), even if we're the ones who gave them life; and we have a glamorous life, even if it looks like eating dinner at the same table every night and parties at home and conversation about what they did in school today; and we have songs, every day, in all the spaces of life, because those songs are the voices of our children, chanting their demands and complaining about their problems and murmuring their "I love yous" when we most need them.

So what if I used to want to be a rockstar and this is all I got?

What I got is love and fun and adventure and life. So much more than I ever dared to dream.

8 Things Kids are Masters at Destroying

Six boys produce a lot of destruction around my house. Everywhere I look, there are nicks in bookshelves and unintended holes in the walls from errant hands or fingers or just curiosity, and there are cracked toilet lids and picture frames that have no more glass and shattered lights that took an accidental knocking.

But the destruction, by far, hits toys the hardest. Mostly because toys are made of paper. Or something similar. They're surely not made of anything durable, like steel. Or iron. Or cement.

I know, I know. If we had toys made of steel or iron or cement, we'd have bigger things to worry about, and besides, boys wouldn't even be able to lift them, which might be my point.

I have no idea what goes through the minds of toy manufacturers when they're building these complicated little things intended for boy play. I imagine it's something like this: "Haha! Finally! Here is something they'll never be able to destroy."

The answer is always False.

My boys get pretty wild and rowdy when they're playing, but, from what I've observed, it's not any more wild and rowdy than their friends, including some girls. Kids play hard. It's their favorite thing to do, and that means that many times, the toys they choose to play with consistently are usually always on their last life. Or maybe they never really had a life in the first place, because as soon as they came home and saw the boys, they gave up (remember the scene in *Toy*

Story 3 when Woody and Buzz and Jessie watch the kids at daycare play with the old toys and you can just tell they're terrified to be brought into the room? That's what I imagine any toys coming into our house feel like, if they have feelings.).

So I'm just putting it out there, toy manufacturers: If you want to test whether or not your product is really durable—and I'm talking nothing-is-going-to-destroy-this durable—send it to my house.

Here are some things we've already tried and successfully destroyed:

1. Anything made of foam.

Once upon a time, my second son got a Thor foam hammer for his birthday. It was the coolest thing, if you talked to him. Two days later, it was about half its original size, with tiny little bite marks all over it, because his little brother thought it looked like a good thing to eat. THIS IS THE ONLY THING FOAM IS GOOD FOR.

Trust me. We made light sabers out of pool noodles this summer, because we thought our boys would really enjoy some safe sword play, except it's hard to sword fight when you're focused on how many bite marks your opponent's light saber has. They kept slashing me in the face, because I couldn't stop staring, marveling at how quickly those cool light sabers had deteriorated.

You know those foam protectors they put on the metal bars of trampolines so kids don't get hurt while they're jumping? Yeah, my little foamivores got those, too. Maybe they'll learn their lesson next time a body part connects with a metal pole. But I doubt it. They'd probably think it was fun and try to do it again.

2. Anything made with a thousand pieces that don't keep their pieces.

This would be things like LEGOs that get opened immediately, without any plan, and dumped out. It was a sad awakening when I realized no one really cares about putting together that awesome Star Wars starship as much as I do. This category also hosts things like puzzles, which are all packaged in a bag kids can't open and neither can parents—so when it is finally, finally, finally wrestled open, the pieces go flying everywhere, and at least one of them is sure to disappear. Forever.

(I think toy manufacturers do this on purpose. Someone somewhere is laughing every time a parent sweats through trying to open something and a billion pieces fly everywhere. You know who's not laughing? Me. Thanks for another anxiety attack, toy manufacturers. My kid just tossed a puzzle into my lap and asked me to open it.)

3. Mr. Potato Head's butt.

This was just lazy designing, in my opinion. I get why it's there—easy storage for all the pieces that make Mr. Potato Head Mr. Potato Head, but it's just that Mr. Potato Head, at least in my house, has a very leaky butt, because every other minute my kids are asking me to put Mr. Potato Head's butt back on, except we don't allow the word "butt" in our house, so it sounds more like, "Can you put Mr. Potato Head's booty back on?" which is really kind of ridiculous and a little bit cute.

I'll put it back on, and then I'll watch them fill it up with pieces and close it and then open it again, and, whoops, there went the butt flap again and all the pieces are spilling out and my kid is throwing Mr. Potato Head across the room, because it's so frustrating. I know, kids. It's frustrating when you have a leaky butt on your hands.

Especially when it's not your own.

4. Action figures.

These guys. I feel sorry for them. They lose limbs like we lose matching shoes. I've found Captain America with only one arm, but "at least he still has his shield," the boys say. I've found Hulk without a head, which would be a very dangerous Hulk, if you ask me. I've found Iron Man missing a leg, but "at least he can still fly."

All I know is I'm hoping they won't come back to avenge their missing limbs, because I have no idea where they are.

5. Games.

Now, I love playing Apples to Apples and Ticket to Ride and Dominion just like any other parent, and even, when it comes to kids' games, Battleship and Candy Land and Operation. It's just that even though these games are super fun and most of my boys are old enough to play them, they come with two thousand tiny pieces. And they're packaged in boxes.

This alone is a recipe for disaster, but put together, it's a recipe for we'll-never-play-this-again. The boys try to cram on the box lid, even though the Battleship board is still halfway open, and the box tears in half, and then the pieces are everywhere, and we have to break out the Duct tape, and even still, pieces go missing. Ever tried to play Operation without the liver and the heart and the funny bone? It's not as much fun. What's even worse, though, is when parents don't replace the batteries (they never do—but that's an essay for another day).

6. Anything that's super cool.

The 8-year-old once got a microscope for his birthday because he was really into science (and still is), but it lasted all of three days, because he left it out on the table once and one of his twin brothers decided to see what would happen if he squeezed the tiny little light bulb. Easy enough to fix, except that when he crushed it with his tiny little hands, he also bent a piece that wouldn't permit any other light bulb to be screwed in. (Fun fact: How many people did it take to screw in a light bulb? About twelve, until Husband looked at it and called it what it was: destroyed.)

The 6-year-old once got a really cool bug catcher that broke the first time a fly got caught. (I know. That wasn't his fault.) Another boy once got a frogosphere where you can raise your own frogs, and we didn't even try that one, because we're talking about live animals. After what these boys do to toys? No thanks. You just dodged a bullet, baby frogs.

7. Scooters.

It's amazing how difficult it is to align the handlebars with the wheels on a scooter when you're putting it together and how amazingly easy it is to mangle this contraption beneath the tires of a minivan when boys forget to put it back where it belongs.

8. Stuffies.

If the 3-year-olds are left alone with a stuffed animal for any amount of time, they will defluff it, which is about as terrible as it sounds. Every now and then they sneak a little stuffy past my eyes and hide it under their pillow until I take a bathroom break from my post right outside their room, which is where I have to stay if there's any chance that they will take a nap, and when I come back, I find miniature throw carpets that have dog heads and lion heads and pink elephant heads with sparkly purple eyes.

In fact, this has happened so often recently I'm considering starting a business selling slippers made from old, defluffed stuffed animals. Because those little throw rugs look suspiciously like the material used for kids slippers. Might as well make a profit off my boys' destruction.

All I'm really trying to say, toy manufacturers, is that you're going to have to do better than this. Let's see you make something cool that will not be taken apart in ten seconds and put back together all wrong, or maybe, worse, better than before. Let's see you make something that can withstand cross-purpose playing (like puppet sticks that are actually durable enough to be used as swords —which will happen in a house of boys). Let's see you make something kids can't destroy.

I know it's a daunting task, but judging by the price of that action hero castle they got for Christmas last year that was destroyed two hours later, I'm paying you about twenty-five dollars an hour. You can do this. I know you can.

Plus, my boy just put a cool Star Wars light saber on his birthday wish list, and I still remember what happened to the last one. No one wants to see an 8-year-old on a war path to figure out who broke his favorite toy. Trust me.

Parenting is Like Living in an Insane Asylum

Sometimes I feel like I'm doing a pretty good job as a parent. Relationships are good, all those consequences we've put into our Family Playbook—a list of infractions and their expected consequences—are well understood, the house is in almost perfect order.

And then my children wake up.

It only takes seconds to realize that they are completely different people today. Not only have they forgotten all the new infractions and consequences we brainstormed yesterday, but they also no longer care about getting to school on time or wearing clean clothes or keeping their room even the slightest bit tidy.

Yesterday my two older boys came down for breakfast fifty minutes before we had to leave for school. Today they were still not eating breakfast ten minutes before we had to walk out the door, and I had to shout my last you're-not-going-to-get-breakfast warning above the volume of an audio book, because I'm too lazy to walk up the stairs for the sixteenth time (I blame my laziness on my broken foot, which happened a week ago when I gracefully fell down our stairs. And Post Traumatic Stress, which I feel every time I approach stairs).

Yesterday they liked the grilled broccoli and cauliflower and carrots we brushed with olive oil and sprinkled with sea salt and roasted in the oven. Today they gagged just looking at them.

Yesterday they all sat perfectly still in their separate spaces while their daddy read two picture books and I read a Narnia chapter book and again while we engaged in our ten minutes of Sustained Silent Reading time and then again while we did our meditation breathing and prayer time. We didn't have to remind them once to get back in their spots or stop talking or that, no, an art journal is not a book you read and, no, the pen in your hand is not necessary during reading time (unless you're taking notes—which he was clearly not). Today they think reading time means chase-your-brother-around-the-library time.

It's enough to drive a parent insane.

I've often joked that parenting is like living in an insane asylum. But the joke is usually true. Insanity, as defined by Albert Einstein, is "doing the same thing over and over again and expecting different results."

THIS IS WHAT KIDS DO, EVERY SINGLE DAY.

They try to write during story time, even though we've told them a billion times it's not allowed. They try to sneak that LEGO toy into the bath tub, thinking this time will surely be different and we won't object. They seem surprised that 8 p.m. is lights out, even though nothing has changed in their thousands of nights.

The problem is, our kids are the least consistent people on the planet. Every single day they wake up completely different people.

The bigger problem, though, is that they give us that one little taste of expectation realization, and we think they CAN sit still for two stories and a chapter book. And we keep expecting it every other day.

For as long as we've had twins, I have fantasized about two boys napping in the same bedroom for more than an hour and a half. We were spoiled, because our older boys took three-hour naps and could be trusted to sleep in their rooms with their doors closed.

The first time we left the twins for three hours with the door closed, they pulled down the forty-four shirts in their closet, painted walls with their poop, and ate the cardboard pages of *Goodnight Moon*.

So the next time I set a timer for two hours (because surely they'd just woken up early) and I sat outside their door to work on some deadline material. I could hear them shrieking, but we'd baby proofed everything, and there were only two mattresses on their floor (not even beds, because the twins could destroy furniture in 3.4 seconds). Nothing they could get into. Nothing that would hurt them. Nothing to occupy them for two hours.

They got really quiet, but I didn't worry. We're all quiet when we're sleeping.

When the timer went off, I opened their door and found them sitting on clouds, all the stuffing ripped out of the lone Beanie Boo someone had left in their room.

The next day, I opened their door. I sat right outside. I corrected them when they so much as moved.

AND THEY FELL ASLEEP. FOR TWO WHOLE HOURS.

Oh, thank God, I said. It *is* possible.

So, of course, the next day, I did the exact same thing. Except as soon as they were asleep, I went to my room to do some more involved work. Two hours later, they had knocked their closet doors off the hinges, strung all their ties from the ceiling fan and neatly lined up their shoes under their mattresses, all with silent feet and hands.

Oh my word.

It's maddening and confusing and impossible to keep up with these every-day-different children. It's impossible to know that today the 8-year-old only got seven hours of sleep but will wake up the happiest kid in the world, but tomorrow he'll get twelve hours of sleep and will wake up gnawing on all the heads he bit off before breakfast. It's impossible to know that today the 6-year-old will follow all the rules and help with everything around the house, and tomorrow he will wake up a defiant little monster. It's impossible to know that today the 4-year-old will love reading those books out loud to me but tomorrow he will wake up acting like he'd rather eat spinach than finish the last five sentences of that *Little Bear* story.

What's a parent to do?

We just keep doing the same thing over and over, expecting different results from this insane asylum. Because, you know. Consistency and all.

Also because sometimes it *does* work, and those times it works might just be enough to power us through the times it doesn't.

And if they're not, well. At least there's red wine. And chocolate.

And a lock on our bedroom door they haven't learned to pick (yet).

The Real Deal (Parenthood Unplugged)

Do I Ever Feel Like Giving Up? Every Other Minute.

A few weeks ago I got a text from my sister, who had her third baby in February. The text said, "Tell me you have days when you just can't handle it. When walking out of the house is all you can do to survive. I just need to hear it from another human."

I laughed out loud, even though I knew she was dead serious. And in my head were responses like "every single day" and "just this morning" and "on a minute-by-minute basis."

Parenting is hard. It's the hardest thing I've ever done, and I used to run six miles every morning in Houston's 10,000-pound humidity before commuting an hour to downtown's *Houston Chronicle* office. I used to marathon-train on ten miles of hills pushing a double baby stroller that carried a 4-year-old and a 3-year-old. I used to work for a narcissist.

Parenting is still the hardest thing I've ever done.

There are so many hours of my day that I just feel like giving up and hitch-hiking to downtown San Antonio's Riverwalk, where Husband and I had a life before children—a life that didn't include a panic attack every time a kid steps too close to the edge of the path and I imagine having to jump into that river's dirty black water to save him.

Like the morning last week, when the 3-year-old twins went outside into our very safe (normally) backyard while I transferred a load of laundry from the washing machine to the dryer. Two minutes, tops. That's all it took. By the time I finished, one of the twins had come back inside, and the whole house smelled like gasoline.

"Why does the house smell like gasoline?" I said, to no one in particular. The twin looked at me. I looked at him. He had his guilty eyes on.

"What were you doing out there?" I said.

"Nuffing," he said.

I knew it was definitely something, because of those guilty eyes. A mom always knows, after all.

His twin brother came in smelling like a gas pump, so I looked out on the deck, where they didn't even have the foresight to hide what they'd been doing. There, on a deck chair, was a gas can their daddy uses to fill up the lawn mower the three times a year he mows. That gas can is stored behind a locked door. A locked and sealed door that somehow, SOMEHOW, these Dennis the Menaces had cracked open in less than two minutes.

They poured gasoline (less than half a gallon, for those who are concerned) all over the back deck, the grass, and themselves. It's a good thing no one in my house smokes, because we all would have been blown to high heaven.

I put them both in the bath (which was not on the schedule for the morning) while the baby stayed downstairs in his jumper seat wailing because he doesn't like to be alone, and washed them, rinsed them, scrubbed them, rinsed them and washed them again. Husband sprayed off the deck (which also wasn't on the schedule for the morning) and saturated all the grass, because a Texas summer hits 4,000 degrees, and we were afraid the sun might make the gasoline-drenched grass spontaneously combust and blow us all to high heaven anyway.

That morning was one of those give-up days, because there's no way to be one step ahead in my house. There's no way I can fully toddler-proof every room. There's no way I can keep them out of every single thing they find to amuse themselves. It would take twenty-three of me, and as far as I know, cloning is considered unethical.

That morning I wanted to walk out and let them fend for themselves in gasoline-scented clothes that spread their stench all over the house in less than two seconds.

I used to feel guilty when feelings like this crept up. I used to beat myself up for sometimes wishing that they just weren't twins, that there weren't two of them ALL THE DANG TIME, that they weren't so insatiably curious and 3 years old and nearly impossible to parent right now.

But there is something important I've learned in my years of parenting: Just because there are moments when we want to run away, when we want to flat-out give up, when we want to trade our challenging kids for easier kids for just this little moment in time so we can catch up and learn to appreciate them again, it doesn't mean that we don't still love them with a love that is never-ending.

These little, irrational humans can be the best and worst people we know on any given day at any given moment.

There are days when I want to sit down and color next to my 3-year-olds, because they've been playing so well together and the morning's disasters have been minimal, and, gosh, I just love them so much, and then there are mornings when I want to put them on Craig's list's free page (I'd have to lie to really sell the idea, though. Something like "Two well behaved twins, of undetermined age." Because what kind of crazy person would want two 3-year-olds voluntarily?)

There are hours when I love to comb through those old picture albums that show these two hooked up to machines because they were premature and remember how I fretted and cried and tried my best to help them learn how to eat, and there are days when those first moments feel like entire lifetimes away from *this* moment, when they stuck their whole arm in the just-used toilet to see what poop floating in pee feels like (They already know. We've done this drill before.).

There are minutes when I pull them into my lap and kiss all over their faces until they're giggling uncontrollably, because they're getting so big and so fun, and then there are minutes when I'm half-heartedly holding their big brother away from them so he doesn't clobber them for marking all over his journal with a giant red permanent marker they found lying around somewhere (who keeps giving us permanent markers? Please stop.).

Parenting is not for the weak. This is the hardest responsibility we will ever have in our lives. Raising another human being to be a decent person is not easy, and there are many times along our journeys when we will feel like giving up and giving in and giving out.

It just comes with the territory.

So I fire off my response to my sweet sister. "Yes," I say. "Just about every day. Doesn't mean you're a bad mother."

Because it doesn't.

These moments when we feel the tension between wanting to give up and knowing we can't make us stronger parents. They make us better people. They drag us into a deeper understanding of love.

Good thing, too. Because my toddler just figured out how to open a can of paint Husband left unguarded and now the pantry wall has a Thermal Spring scribble-masterpiece drying on it.

I'm going to be one amazing person by the time this is all over.

How to Know You're on the Right Track as a Parent

There's this school of thought that really bothers me. It shakes fingers at us and says that if we think parenting is hard or we feel like giving up on a daily or hourly or minute-by-minute basis or we, God forbid, wish our kids would be different, less difficult people for a fleeting moment in time, then we probably shouldn't have become parents in the first place.

It's a lie.

It's a dangerous lie, too, one that keeps us locked in chains as parents, because that's when we start looking around at all those people who make it look so easy, who make it look as though they're enjoying every single minute of every single in-the-trenches hour, and we can think that we are somehow deficient in our parenting abilities.

You know what the easy part of parenting is? Making it look easy.

You know what the hard part of parenting is? Every other second.

Parenting is hard. You'll never hear me say it's easy. It's hard because I work really hard at it. And, also, nothing worthwhile is ever easy.

I fail every single day at this parenting gig. Every single day. Sometimes that failing looks like yelling because the 3-year-olds just poured a whole package of brand new crayons out on the table and broke twenty-six of them in half before I could even get to them, even though I just got done telling them to leave the crayons alone until their brothers got home. Sometimes that failing looks like speaking more sharply than I intended to the 8-year-old because I just warned him not to swing the broom like that, and he decided to do it anyway, and he broke a light. Sometimes it looks like standing in a kitchen and crying without being able to say why I'm crying, just knowing there are too many voices and too many words and too many needs knocking all at once, and it's overwhelmingly suffocating.

But I will never pretend I don't fail, because it's not true. I will never pretend that parenting my six boys is not hard, because it's not true. The world is not served by facades and pretty little pictures and perfect little examples. The world is served by imperfection and being brave enough to bare it.

So, yeah, parenting feels hard to me. It's not because I don't love my children. I love them with a love that is great and deep and wild enough to gouge out whole parts of me that never belonged. They are precious and wonderful and most of all beloved.

Parenting feels hard because I'm trying, every day, to be better at it than I was yesterday. It feels hard because we're all people and we're all imperfect and we are living and growing together in ways that can grind and carve and shape. It feels hard because these are tiny little humans we're talking about, tiny little humans who will one day become men and women, and we get to shepherd them into that, and it is a giant, humbling, magnanimous task. A privilege. But a mountain of responsibility.

I don't take it lightly.

I would venture to say that if parenting feels easy every second of every day, if there is never a moment where we feel like locking ourselves in a bathroom for just a breath or fifty of them, if we never wish, for that tiny split of a split-second, that they would be different people, we are probably doing it wrong.

The best parts of life demand hard work and dedication and perseverance, and the things most worth doing will, at any moment in time, feel hard. That's how I know I'm on the right track as a parent.

For me, parenting feels hard every time my 8-year-old forgets how he's been taught to handle his anger and lashes out with hands instead of words, because he's always been a gifted kid whose emotional development lags behind others his age, and we've worked really, really hard trying to walk him toward a place of control and knowledge and healthy expression of all the emotions, not just the good ones, and sometimes it all feels like a losing battle. It feels hard when I remember what a brilliant and kind and loving little boy he is and how much good he has the potential to blast into the world, if only he didn't have this one little thing. It feels hard when I see that school number on my cell, and I wonder if it's him they're calling about.

Parenting feels hard every time the 3-year-olds eat a tube of toothpaste and leave the evidence on the counter, because I have to choose not to yell and use my words in ways that will honor and teach and show grace and love even in this discipline moment that's happened a billion times already. It feels hard when the 6-year-old wakes up on a school morning and barfs all over the Hot Wheels the 3-year-olds dumped out, not just because now it means cleaning up puke, but also because no mother wants to see her baby sick. It feels hard every time the 5-year-old comes home from school and talks about how one of the boys in his class was mean to him on the playground, because then I just want to throat punch the bullying kid, but I have to talk to my boy about how the people who choose to bully often don't know any better and need to be shown a better way of making friends, and he's the one who will have to do this brave and kind and world-changing work.

Parenting feels hard when they forget who they are. It's hard because I love them so much, because I want to order their worlds just so, because I want to make their decisions for them, because I don't want to sit by and watch those consequences break their hearts, but I have to, because it's the only way they'll learn and grow and stumble back to who they are.

Sometimes I don't feel up to this task. Sometimes I don't feel equipped. Sometimes I want to give up, but I also know that I'm a fighter. I persevere. I keep going. Which is kind of the point of all this parenting in the trenches—to show us what we're made of. And you know what? I'm made of some pretty tough stuff.

So, no, I'm not going to suck it up, buttercup, because I have discovered something else in my eight years with these delightful little boys. Parenting is hard because I'm doing it right. Because I fail. Because they fail. Because we keep going, all of us together, along the road toward wholehearted living.

There is nothing greater in the world than this.

6 Annoying Things Kids Will Never Understand

The other day I was trying to put my 3-year-old in the car, and we were in a hurry. I wanted to get to the grocery store and back before it was time for their lunch, since you definitely DO NOT want to be caught out in public when two headstrong 3-year-olds and a 9-month-old decide they're hungry and you're not feeding them fast enough, because, look, we're surrounded by food and all you have to do is BUY SOMETHING FOR THEM.

That's a fight I didn't want to have today. So I was doing my best to buckle the 3-year-old quickly and make sure the chest piece was positioned in the exact place it should be, because I'm all about safety, while he was more concerned with waving a book he'd found in my face.

"Look, Mama," he kept saying over and over and over again. Wave, wave, wave.

"I'm trying to buckle you," I said, ducking.

"But look what I found," he said, still waving it in my face. I took the book and threw it down on the floor of the van.

"Stop putting the book in my face," I said. "I don't like it when you shove things in my face."

He ignored me, of course, because he's a 3-year-old and that's what 3-year-olds do, and he replaced a book with his finger, which I know I just saw up his nose. It took a few impressive Matrix moves that I'm still feeling today to get out of that sticky spot, and then he was buckled and we were on our merry way, my annoyance dissipating with every mile we logged, replaced by anxiety and dread, because who in their right mind takes two 3-year-olds and a 9-month-old to a grocery store? I was totally setting myself up for failure, and I knew it.

But I distracted myself by thinking about how kids probably don't even understand the whole concept of "I don't like having things shoved in my face," because they don't realize they're shoving anything in a face. They're just trying to get our attention. It's how they communicate.

I know, because I watched them after we got home from the store (which I don't want to talk about, so don't even ask). The two 3-year-olds were talking to each other, and one would hold a train right up into the face of the other one and say, "I want this one. Do you want this one?" Twin 1 was trying to pick a fight, but Twin 2 wasn't taking the bait, mostly because he couldn't see the train that was right up in his face. It was too close. So he just ignored it and said, "No," and went right on playing.

There are so many things that kids don't understand. Take, for instance, the "please don't put your stinky feet on me."

First of all, kids don't even know what stinky smells like. They sort of know stinky when it comes to things like farts and skunk smell and food they don't like, but when it comes to anything connected to their body, stinky is not a word in their vocabulary. They will come in from playing outside in the middle of a Texas summer and smell like a whole pasture full of cows and dung and the dog that was dispatched to round up all the strays that need milking, even though we don't live anywhere near cows. They will fight to the death about taking a bath, no matter how many times we tell them that the smell they keep looking around trying to find is actually them.

Every night at dinner, the 9-year-old, without even thinking, will put his stinky feet, which have been trapped inside his tennis shoes all day, on my legs. All over them, actually. He moves them up and down and side to side, because he has trouble sitting still after all that over-stimulation at school. I can practically see the fumes swirling up from his black socks with the neon green toes, and those fumes get to be rubbed all over my legs. Just what I wanted.

He does it because he's not thinking and because he loves me, but THIS IS NOT LOVE. Trust me. It's dinnertime, and all I can smell is Fritos mixed with pinto beans and really aged cheese, even though what we're having is salmon with salad.

Kids also don't understand things like "Please give me some personal space," because what is personal space to kids? They will touch me and prod me and lean into me and not think twice about it. They will stand so close to me I'll trip over them on my way to get some requested milk. They will fall all over each other and think it's hilarious instead of annoying. They will cling to my legs on the walk to school or, worse, walk in step directly in front of me and then, when they've disappeared from my view because there's a baby strapped to my frontside, they will stop, and my Matrix move skills will be tested once more as I try to stop myself from tripping over them and falling, and I'll be sore for another month.

"I would like to go to bed" is probably the most misunderstood phrase in our house. To our kids, this means, "I would like you to come into our room a thousand times seeking extra hugs and kisses and to especially tell us in no less than one thousand words what your brother just did to you." Just when we're falling into dreamland and it's looking like the most beautiful place we've ever seen, someone will knock on our door with something important to tell us, like how he thinks that tomorrow is crazy sock day and he doesn't have any crazy socks, so can he borrow some, and it will take us five more hours to get back to sleep.

"I would like to go to bed" is also code for "You can totally get out of your bed and take all the books down from the library shelves," if you're asking our 3-year-old twins, which is why we use a locking doorknob installed backwards on their room and lock them in it at night, because 3-year-olds roaming the house at night is scarier than that freaky doll Chucky coming for a visit with his eyes that never blink.

"Chew with your mouth closed" looks like a 3-year-old trying to figure out how in the world you're supposed to chew food when you close your mouth, looking confusedly at all his brothers who have mastered the talent and then, after rolling the food around his mouth with his tongue, opting to swallow it whole so he chokes on a stump of unchewed broccoli.

"You're not hungry; you're just bored," gets me tagged as the "worst mother ever." And "That's not in our budget right now" results in a boy fetching my wallet, pulling out a credit card and saying, "Then use this," reminding me that I need to teach him about responsible use of credit cards, because society's claws are thick.

So maybe things get a little lost in translation, but the truth is I'm kind of glad. Because the times I feel really annoyed that a kid is waving something in my face and I've already asked him to stop once are the moments I remember how these translation errors are all places where I get to consider things from their point of view and I get to remember what it was like to be a kid and I get to take a deep, long breath and hope I'm breathing in patience and not more boiling annoyance (or stinky feet). And then I get to be a good mother who teaches and directs and walks them toward a deeper understanding of what it means to be human.

But, seriously, if you don't get your stinky feet off me…

Don't Judge Me By the State of My Yard. I'm a Parent.

Not too long ago, one of our neighbors was selling his house. We saw the sign but didn't think much of it. It didn't involve us. At least that's what we thought.

And then one night, when we were out running wild in the cul-de-sac with our children, he followed his daughter out the door, presumably to watch her play. Except he headed straight for Husband and said, "Hey man, we need to do something about your bush."

No preamble, no how are you, no small talk. Just straight to the point. I guess I kind of like that. I'm not much for small talk, either.

Husband and I both knew what bush he was talking about.

This bush is not really a bush at all. It's just a plant. Every spring it blooms with beautiful orange flowers that brighten up the yard, and it keeps growing and growing and growing until it dies off in winter. Then it leaves its dried-out stems—that, by this time, look like trunks—in our little flower garden unless someone makes the effort to trim them. Every spring it grows back with a vengeance, offering its green and orange around all the dead parts that someone still hasn't trimmed.

The problem isn't that all those dead parts make this beautiful plant look ugly. It's that when the neighbors' trash blows out of their over-filled trash cans when they're sitting out for trash pickup, this massive plant likes to eat it. And whoever is supposed to be trimming the dead stems also isn't picking out of its clutches all the nasty pieces of other people's trash.

Oh, wait. That's supposed to be me.

There are some things you just give up on when you have as many kids as we do (Okay, many things. Lots of things. A whole life of things.). Like the yard. And a clean house. And spontaneously eating out for dinner. But that's beside the point.

At any rate, this neighbor needed us to do something about that plant, because he was selling his house, and this plant was making his home value plummet.

I totally understand. I know we can't control who our neighbors are, and our poor neighbors just happened to move next to the family with six boys and two parents who are ~~drowning~~ doing just fine.

We planted this flower garden back when we only had one child and one more on the way and life seemed so easy. We thought (such innocent kids we were) that we'd be able to manage. We'd be able to keep up with weeding and trimming back and watering. We would keep our yard pretty.

Turns out six kids 8 years old and younger keep you really, really, really busy, and one of the things that falls from the idealistic we-can-handle-this list is, unfortunately, yard work.

It isn't even because we're lazy. It's mostly because boys make it impossible to have a nice yard.

Case in point: The other day, my 5-year-old came to me with a digging spade. "I'm just going to dig a hole in the front yard so I can bury something," he said, already walking out the door.

I caught his arm. "Wait a minute," I said. "You're what?"

"I'm going to dig a hole and bury something," he said, as if this was a perfectly reasonable thing to do.

"What are you going to bury?" I said, because I wasn't at all surprised by the first part.

"Nothing," he said, but I saw what was in his hands. His brother's favorite Hot Wheels car.

And then, when I was helping Husband save the grass from the gasoline my 3-year-olds dumped all over the backyard, my 8-year-old came out to the back deck and said, "I just planted some cucumbers and carrots out front. So we'll have a vegetable garden."

Um.

I now have renegade plants that are clearly not flowers growing in the flower garden I haven't weeded in two years.

Another part of the problem is that every time we plan on having a yard work day, something else comes up. Something else like two 3-year-olds deciding they're going to pull down all the clothes in their closet, even though they'd have to be Spider-Man to reach them now with all the creative safeguards we've put in their room (I don't even know. I think the Avengers lost a couple of players.). Something else like the 6-year-old deciding he's going to get into the art cabinet during Quiet Time to cut up some tiny little squares of paper he'll later put in a container and dump out on someone's head in the front yard because he thinks it's funny (So not). Something else like the 8-year-old deciding he wants to find out if a pumpkin will grow in the old tree graveyard beside the house.

This is how we got to be the terrible neighbors whose house

looks like an orphanage. ("How many kids live there?" I imagine the people who walk their dogs in our cul-de-sac say. "We're not really sure," their walking partner answers.) Scooters crop up in the clearly dying grass; the herb garden off to the side is courting a weed tree, because I cannot even; and the boys ask to go gather wildflowers in our yard because it's a whole wildflower field ("I brought some flowers for you, Mama," the 3-year-olds say. "Thank you for weeding the yard," I say.).

I know what you're thinking. Why not just hire a lawn crew and take care of it the easy way? Well, my question to you is, have you ever tried to feed six boys who are always, always hungry? There's your answer.

Also, one of these days we're going to have a yard-working force, with six boys weeding and mowing and tidying up and trimming bushes and gathering herbs, and then our house is going to be the envy of the block. But for now it most definitely looks like six children live here. Maybe more (because twins).

The thing is, when you're a parent, some things have to slide until you can get your head above water (which is probably never. We're all just lying to ourselves.). Our head hasn't been above water for quite a while now, because there are six of them and only two of us, and they're still young. That's okay. It's what we signed up for. I'm not complaining. I don't really care about our yard, truth be told.

If you accidentally bought a house next to us, I'm just warning you now, when it's too late, that we're not going to be winning "best block in the neighborhood" anytime soon, and it's mostly our fault. Sorry if we're ruining hopes and dreams by being the weakest link. We just have better things to do. Like setting our kids free out front on a summer evening and playing an epic game of chase on scooters and roller blades that your kids will join in (you're welcome).

Chances are, next time you stop by my door, you'll have to step over a scooter obstacle course just to make it to the doorbell, because boys are really bad about putting them away where they belong. So watch your step (and maybe take a couple on your way out to teach them a lesson in natural consequences).

We're really awesome people once you get past the trash cans that are perpetually left between our vehicle and our garage (lifting the garage door is too much work when you've been wrestling six kids into bed) and the grass that's always just a little bit (or maybe a lot) higher than the two inches it's supposed to be and the bushes that look like bears might live inside.

If you're judging us by the state of our front yard, you'll never get to know that.

Thanks for cutting us some slack. You'll be glad you did.

How My Boys Try (And Fail) to Use the Force

Husband and my older boys have lately been trying to cram in some viewings of old Star Wars movies, because, I don't know, fake visual effects and all. It's important, Husband says, to introduce them to Luke and Yoda and Hans and, most of all, The Force. It's not important, however, to introduce them—especially the one who wants to be a filmmaker—to blobs that look like someone took a bunch of fake dog poop, painted it green, and turned it into a pile, but no one's listening to me.

I see Husband's point. I mean, I remember watching all the Star Wars movies as a kid and enjoying the story, because it's a good one, and even thinking that maybe, just maybe The Force was real, and I could one day do what Luke Skywalker did, if I could only find a light saber.

It's just that when he says it's important to *introduce* the boys to The Force, I take exception. Because my boys are already well-acquainted with The Force. It's what they use to

1. Get their clothes in the laundry hamper...or not.

I know, I know. All the times I've come across their renegade pieces of clothing, smashed right up against a laundry hamper, it's just because they're still not that great at using The Force to get their clothes *inside* it. They only need a little more practice. That's all. And when I come across a shirt or some pants or a pair of underwear—clean? Dirty? I'm not checking—on the couch or their bedroom floor or in the bathroom sink, it's probably because one of their brothers did an arm fart in the middle of their putting-away-my-clothes-by-using-The-Force practice, and they dissolved into hysterical laughter, which threw their aim off. Fewer distractions, they need.

2. Put their dirty bowls, silverware and plates in the sink…or not.

It doesn't matter if they've had three times every day for the last eight years to practice this skill, it's a really tough one to learn. I can understand that. Some things take time. Lots of time. I realize they really, really, really want to get those bowls and silverware and plates in the sink, but The Force, at least the one they're working with at this moment in time, isn't strong enough to even pick them up off the table. Maybe The Force doesn't work as well when it comes to wood tables and food. Force interference, they are.

3. Turn off lights…or not.

I get that this is a tricky thing to do, that flicking a finger from across the room to turn the light off in the last room they left. I'm sure The Force employs some intricately designed movement that requires motor skills my boys haven't acquired yet, because every time I pass their rooms at any time of the day, the light is blazing and no one's home. When I point out the left-on light, they act like they forgot, but that's just a ruse, because males don't always like admitting to what they can't yet do (I know, because the lights are always on in every room Husband leaves, too, and it was never him). Better honed motor skills, this task requires.

4. Set the table…or not.

I'm sure this goes back to The Force not working when it comes to things like wood tables and food, or forks and spoons and plates, because every time I ask one of them to set the table so I can finish up dinner, I turn around to put all those pots and pans of steaming deliciousness on the table, and there are no plates and forks and spoons with which to eat, and my boys are all in the living room reading or building a block tower or banging out an original melody on the piano, as if they thought this job was already done. Different kind of Force, this entails.

5. Shut the door…or not.

You would think this might be the easiest of them all. Go out the door, pull The Force along with you. Come inside, fling The Force behind you. But I guess I have some young Padawans who haven't quite made it to Jedi status, because most of time, when they're coming in or out, they don't even seem to notice the door standing ajar and all the flies following them in. I wish there were a Force that could beat the flies, because they seem to love our house. So much so that the 6-year-old wrote an essay in school about how if he had a pet, it would be a fly-eating frog so it could catch all the flies his mom hates. Which is why I really want my kids to master this closing-the-door-using-The-Force, because we don't need kids' teachers to know about things like that. More Physical Force, I demand.

6. Wash their bodies…or not.

I really wish I could help them here. If only words could pull enough of The Force with them to lather up the kids in the bath. Because "make sure it's the first thing you do" is the same thing I say every single night when they get in the bath, and when that timer clangs and I tell them it's time to get out, their hair isn't even wet. I know they're really trying to use The Force in between driving that Hot Wheels car up the sides of the bath tub and pretending they're swimming in deep water. It's not an easy thing to tell them it's just not working, but somebody's gotta do it. Intensified training, they need.

7. Put away the laundry…or not.

Oh, wait. That's me. This the one time The Force actually works for my boys, even if it ends up piling underwear in a closet and shoving hang-up shirts in the pajama drawer and crumpling jeans in the underwear drawer. I don't even care. At least The Force put it all away. Better than I'm doing, it is.

Well. Now that I've written all of that out, I can better understand where my little Padawans are coming from. They just need a more skilled Jedi Master to help them hone their powers and teach them the intricate subtleties of using The Force.

Since it's clear that The Force doesn't work for Husband, either, I guess that means I signed up to be their Yoda. To work, I go.

When You Reach THAT Point in Pregnancy

We are eagerly awaiting the arrival of our sixth (and last) baby, another boy, and I have reached THAT point in pregnancy.

There comes THAT point in every pregnancy, when the days feel like they're two thousand hours long because of the other littles demanding time and attention, and the nights feel like they're four thousand hours long because you're staring at a clock, hoping, hoping, hoping you can just, for once, for these last few days, fall asleep and stay asleep, since there is no promise of that once a baby comes.

You know you have solidly reached THAT point in pregnancy when:

You can't turn over at night without moaning at the pain of trying.

You wake your husband and ask him to give you a little push, because you're stuck on your back and you're starting to panic and there's the vena cava, and why do you suddenly feel so lightheaded?

You get up to go to the bathroom forty times a night, and every single time you wish you had a walker to lean on, because your back seized up while you were lying down and you can't move your legs now.

In fact, every time you sit for longer than fifteen minutes, you wish you had a walker. Or a wheelchair. Or maybe a fancy stroller.

Your back feels like every bone is broken and every muscle is torn in half.

When your partner complains about how much his back hurts, you snap, "Oh, please. Don't even talk to me about a backache." Because he really has no idea.

Every time you sneeze, you pee a little. Every time you laugh, you pee a little. Every time you choke on the water that went down your throat the wrong way, you pee a little.

Your children tell you your belly is the biggest thing they've ever seen. Bigger than the moon and the basketball they played with in P.E. today and even bigger than the sumo boppers they got for Christmas.

Your belly is so big it forgets how to hold itself and starts sagging toward the floor.

You're bent at a 45-degree angle (backwards) to counterbalance the baby weight on your front side.

You actually practice labor squats, bearing the hip pain, because surely the weight of the baby will break your water instead of your back like it's been doing up until now.

You pull a muscle trying to walk up the stairs.

You dream of running.

You wonder if running might induce labor.

You seriously consider going for a run.

You try to do your pregnancy yoga, and you get stuck on the floor.

You comb your closet for clothes that still fit, a shirt that at least covers your dropping belly, but there is nothing. So you tie a few scarves around your middle. They double as a belly bra, anyway.

You can no longer see your feet on the next step in front of you when you're coming down the stairs, so you just hope you don't miss one.

You nearly face plant when you trip going up the stairs (because you also can't see your feet going up) and run the rest of the way, trying to keep your top-heavy balance, and then you laugh hysterically when it's all over because you didn't just die. Maybe you actually induced labor.

You can't even pretend you're a peppy, beautiful pregnant woman anymore (if you ever were. You're not convinced.). You can't rally. You can only drag.

You waddle without even realizing it until your partner (or, worse, one of your kids) kindly points it out.

You can't reach the silverware at the bottom of your sink without standing on your tiptoes, setting your belly on the counter and then hunching down to pick them up.

Your laptop will no longer fit on your lap.

You burn your stomach trying to cook grilled cheese sandwiches.

You dream about running (did I already say that?).

Pregnancy is a wonderful, beautiful time, until those last brutal weeks, when we vow to never, ever, ever do this again, never ever. But then it will be over and we'll have a tiny precious baby in our arms, and we'll fall so deeply and irreversibly in love we'll forget.

And it's necessary to forget. Of course it is. Who in their right minds would do it all again? But sometimes it's also necessary to remember, so we can keep that last-one vow, for whatever reason it needs to be kept.

So this is my reminder. Last one.

What Every Parent of Twins Needs to Survive

I don't know if I've ever faced a harder challenge in my parenting years than raising twins.

Maybe it's because our twins came near the end of the line of boys and they see all their older brothers do, and they expect that life will be exactly like that for them.

Except there are two of them.

Oh, you want to drink out of a big-boy cup because your older brother did it when he was 2? I'm sorry. There are two of you. You want to sit free at the table instead of strapped into your chairs because all your brothers did it when they were almost 3? I'm sorry. There are two of you. What? You want me to leave the baby gate on your door open because you haven't yet figured out how to climb over it (it's coming)? I'm sorry. In case you haven't noticed, THERE ARE TWO OF YOU.

Our twins are identical, two sides of the same egg. Nature's gift, doctors say. One is left-handed, one is right-handed. They complete each other.

That's part of the problem. What one doesn't think of, the other does. What one is afraid to do, the other will try. It's like having four toddler wrecking balls walking around the house, scheming about what they can destroy next. I imagine their conversations go a little something like this:

Twin 1: Hey. Hey, brother. Mama's not watching. Remember how she told us not to touch this computer? She'll never know if we do. Where is she?

Twin 2: She's in the bathroom. Remember what we did last time she was in the bathroom?

Twin 1: Oh, man. That was fun. But back to this computer. She'll never know. I just can't figure out how to open it.

Twin 2: Like this. But how do you turn it on?

Twin 1: Easy. I've seen Daddy press this button right here.

Twin 2: There it is.

[Mama comes back into the room with the baby she just changed.]

Twin 1: Close it, close it, close it!

Twin 2: Walk away. Not too fast, not too slow. Just enough to look like we weren't doing anything. And make sure you wear the wide eyes. She thinks they're cute.

I love my twins. Of course I do. It's just that they were completely unexpected.

If I could have read a primer two years ago, this is what it might have said: Every parent of twins needs…

1. An extra dose of patience.

You will need this for many things. You will need it for the stranger at the store who asks to see your amazing bundles of joy and, after looking at their angelic sleeping faces, declares she "always wanted twins" and you want to say, "Oh, really? Then take mine," because one was up screaming at 3 a.m. and as soon as you got him calmed down two hours later the other one woke up screaming, and as soon as you got that one calmed down an hour later all the other boys were up asking for breakfast. Which woke up the twins, who were also hungry. Again.

You will need this extra dose of patience for when they learn to talk and there are so.many.words and so.many.whys and so many demands for everything under the sun. You will need it for the potty training and the big-boy-bed transitions and the constant fighting from dawn until dusk.

You will need it for the times you were helping one out of his pajamas and into his day clothes and you return back downstairs to find all the jackets removed from your poetry books and spread across the living room floor like a special carpet for toddler feet, for the six thousandth time (You should probably just put those books away, Mama. Far, far away.).

2. Good decision-making skills.

These will come into play those times they both wake up at 3 a.m. because they're hungry. Which one do you feed first? (Answer: You'll figure out a way to feed both.)

You'll need these skills when one twin is in the downstairs bathroom playing with a plunger in a potty you specifically remember your older boy didn't flush five minutes ago when he stunk it up and the other is in his bathroom upstairs finger painting the mirror with a whole tube of eco-friendly toothpaste. Which do you get first? (Answer: The toilet one. Toothpaste is much easier to clean than the mess an overzealous plunger in a pile of poo can make.)

You'll need them when the one who's known for wandering does exactly that, moves from his nap time place while you take a minute or five for a shower, because it's been four days since the last one, and you walk out to find him playing with the computer he's been told 50 billion times to leave alone and, in his panic to close it, he deletes the

1,500 words you wrote this morning before kids got up. What do you do? (Answer: Cry.)

3. A rigorous workout regimen.

When one is running down the street because someone forgot to lock the deadbolt he can't reach and another is going out back without shoes in 26-degree rain, you'll want to be in tip-top shape for that. I recommend interval training. That way when they stop and change directions, you'll be ready. You've done this a thousand times. Ski jumps. Football runs. All-out sprints.

When they slip, unnoticed (because they're like ninjas), into the playroom while you're wiping down the table after a ridiculously messy lunch, and both of them come out with their scooters, you'll want to be able to wrestle those "cooters" from screaming, flailing bodies without hurting anyone.

And when one collapses in the middle of the park because it's time to go and he's not ready yet and the other thinks that just might work, you'll need strong arms to carry thirty-two pounds of kicking and screaming twins back to the car, one tucked under each armpit.

4. Containment measures.

This would be things like strollers until they're 3 and booster seats until they're 4 and a baby gate on their door until they're…15. Well, maybe 13.

It also means leashes at the city zoo on a packed day, even though you said you'd never use them and you can feel the disapproval of other people and you want to say, "Come talk to me when you have 2-year-old twins. These things have saved their lives 17 billion times, and that was before we even got out of the parking lot."

Containment saves lives. And sanity.

Twins are great. And hard. And maddening. And great. And so hard.

They can disassemble an 8-year-old's room of LEGO Star Wars ships in 3.1 seconds. They can disassemble a heart with one identical smile and a valiant try at saying "Uptown funk you up" that sounds like it should have come with a bleep.

There's just nothing like them in the world. You'll be so glad you get to be their mama.

Especially after they fall asleep.

That Frightening Time When Your Kid is Learning Autonomy

It's a celebratory day when kids are able to buckle their own seat belts and pour their own glasses of milk and bathe themselves and cook their own food (wait, when does this happen again? I'M READY ANYTIME, KIDS).

When they're little, we spend so much of our days doing every single thing for them that every tiny little mastery feels like a major victory.

But in order for them to learn how to do things for themselves, in order for them to achieve autonomy, there is this frightening limbo between beginning and mastering when we must let them practice.

I say it's frightening, because I know. Here's what working toward autonomy looks like in our home:

Pouring milk

The 8-year-old: Check the level on the milk. If it's less than half-filled, overcorrect, because you got this. If it's too full, try anyway, and spill a whole ocean where you can let your Lego man swim before you try to clean it up, because, well, it's fun. And by cleaning it up, you mean wiping it toward the floor so it soaks not only the counter but inside the drawers and cabinets, too. Conveniently forget to clean up the spills you can't see so your mom will find them —not with her eyes, but with her nose—three days later.

The 5-year-old: Only pour from a gallon that is less than half-filled, because you're careful like that.

The 4-year-old: Pour anytime you feel like it, but do it from the floor. Wipe up the mess you've made with a paper towel but no cleaner so the stickiness will steal someone's socks tomorrow. Laugh hysterically when it does.

Tying shoes

The 8-year-old: Tie one, and then get really frustrated when the other one doesn't tie as easily because everyone is talking. Tell everyone to be quiet so you can concentrate and then try again. Tell them to quit looking at you. Make three good attempts, and then take off your shoe that just won't tie today and throw it across the room. Say you'll go to school with only one shoe on. You don't care. Change your mind five minutes before you're supposed to leave, after you've forgotten where the offending shoe landed when you threw it. Your dad will find it and help you put it on. Unless you call him a git (British term, mildly derogatory, made popular by Harry Potter. Means "a foolish or contemptible person").

The 5-year-old: Don't even try. Your mom will do it.

Packing up

8-year-old: Look in your room for your agenda. Complain that you can't find it, even though it's sitting just beside your desk, right by the four thousand Lego pieces you dumped out last night and "forgot" to clean up. Say it's gone forever. Say someone must have stolen it. Say you'll never be able to write down your school assignments again. Ever. Say "You must have moved it," when your mom comes downstairs with it.

5-year-old: Let your mom know you can't find your red folder, then laugh when she pulls it out from under your lunch box, the same place it always is in the mornings, because it's waiting for you to pack it up.

Sweeping the floor

8-, 5- and 4-year-olds: Only sweep a square area of four tiles across and four tiles down. Don't even try to get under the table, where all the food is. It's too hard, and your knee is hurting. You think you might have broken it.

Wiping the table

8-, 5- and 4-year-olds: Use the sponge to push all the extra food to the floor. Be sure to leave streaks all over the table because you didn't want to use the cleaner OR leave a lake because you had a little too much fun spraying the cleaner and the sponge is too soaked to absorb any more excess.

Doing dishes

8-, 5- and 4-year-olds: All the silverware must fit into as few slots as possible, even though there are six slots and three that are still empty. There is no rhyme or reason to putting dishes in; just throw them randomly in whatever space is available. After all, the dishwasher is like a car wash for plates and bowls. Don't worry, Mama. It'll all get clean.

Putting laundry away

8-year-old: Hanging clothes don't have to be hung up, exactly. They can be stuffed into the underwear drawer, because it's not full, and all the other random empty drawers in the room.

5-year-old: Don't pay attention to the labels your mom put up in the closet. Just put your clothes wherever you feel like putting them, even though you share your closet with two other brothers. That way, when you dress for school, you'll have a legitimate reason for dressing in a shirt two sizes too large. "It was on my side," you'll say.

4-year-old: Get mad trying to hang up shirts, and throw your hangers across the floor so some of them break and your parents will help you hang up the rest.

2-year-olds: Rearrange (and by rearrange, you mean empty) the pajama drawer eight times a day because your parents let you put clothes in it once.

Putting on shoes

2-year-olds: It doesn't matter if shoes don't match or if they're different sizes. Just put them on. Shoes are shoes are shoes. Stop trying to match them and put them on the right feet, parents.

Cleaning your room

8-year-old: Make sure all the books that are supposed to go on the bookshelves in your room end up on your bed instead. That way your mom won't be able to find the library books when they're due. Push everything else in the closet and shut the door. You don't need the closet anyway, now that all your clothes are stuffed in drawers.

Bathing

8-, 5- and 4-year-olds: You really only need to wash your hair, your belly and your feet. Everything else is already magically clean.

Dressing

8-year-old: Who cares if the sweatpants you're wearing aren't yours but belong to your 2-years-younger brother and look more like capris than pants? They were in your room, stuffed in a drawer, so they're obviously YOURS. Make sure you leave your pajamas on the floor so they won't make it into the laundry and you can complain two days after laundry day that you don't have any more pajamas. Also, make sure you forget to put your shoes on before getting in the car, because you just know there's a pair in the car (there isn't). And don't check to be sure until you arrive at your destination.

I know that eventually they will get good at all this, because practice makes perfect.

Right?

What I Love About My Large Family

In a world full of three- and four-member families, our eight-member one often draws interesting looks when out in public, especially when the curious onlookers figure out that those six children are really six boys and zero girls.

When we first started building our family, we did not set out planning for a larger-than-average one. It's just that one boy led to another, and before we knew it, we had six of them destroying our home and filling our rooms with laughter and energy and joy.

A large family is challenging in many ways. But it's also wonderful in many other ways. Here are some of the things I love most about our large family:

1. More brains mean more possibilities.

Our family holds a weekly Family Council meeting, where we discuss what we did well as a family the previous week and how we can improve in the upcoming week. We brainstorm solutions to problems we have, like boys taking off clothes and leaving them where they stripped and getting out of bed too many times when it's not an emergency and not being as kind to one another as we should be. All these brains think of solutions one brain could never have generated on its own, and we are all learning to listen to differing perspectives and viewpoints and solutions in a way that is respectful and honoring and celebratory.

We brainstorm Family Time (the hour after dinner) activities together. We create stories together. We decorate for birthday parties together. We laugh about the so-different ways our brains work, and our boys are learning that not one of us thinks the same way or creates the same way or even loves the same way. They are learning acceptance and appreciation and love, right here in these earliest relationships, and this is beautiful to watch unfold.

2. Indulgence is impossible.

I hesitate to say anything is impossible, but this…it just is. We live on a tight budget, which means kids don't get whatever they ask for. When they come home talking about how all their friends have the latest and greatest, we get to talk to them about money and the difference between needs and wants and the necessity of having a budget. They have learned the value of "No, it's not in our budget right now" (which is how we choose to talk with our children about money because we believe it promotes a healthier relationship than "We can't afford it."), and when they see something in a store that they really, really want, they don't pitch a fit when they can't have it —because they have learned the limits of Mama and Daddy's pocketbook.

We have chosen to give our children, as young as they are, a small allowance every month, and if they want to purchase something that costs more than that allowance, they know they must save. The oldest, who is 7, is saving a few dollars every month to buy a German Shepherd puppy.

Saving and spending teaches our children the value of what they have, because they will know it has been bought with a price—at the expense of something else they may have wanted. Like a bug-eyed Beanie Boo. Or a box of LEGOs. Or some chocolate for their dear mother.

3. Sharing is expected.

Our boys know that whatever they get will be shared with their siblings. We enforce a "recipient gets to play with it exclusively" for the first day of receiving, and then it's fair game for everyone. It doesn't always work, of course, because there are days I'll hear the 3-year-old tell his two little brothers, "Hey, stay away, twins," because he's hoarding all those Hot Wheels cars he wants to play with but can't possibly move all at the same time, but they are daily learning the wonder of engaging in shared play instead of mine-and-yours play.

Not only this, but our boys know what it means to share time with Mama and Daddy. We parents can often beat ourselves up about "neglecting" one child over another in certain seasons of neediness, but sharing time is important for children, because they learn that the entire world doesn't revolve around them, that others' needs might trump theirs for a time. They learn they will be okay, that they can do hard things, that they are still loved.

4. Everyone is responsible for their own…everything.

The reality is, there is not enough of their daddy and me to go around most days (when our twins were born, we had four children 2 and younger), which means the 4-year-old could dress himself as soon as he turned 3 and the 3-year-old learned how to put on shoes at 2 and the 7-year-old knows he must keep track of all the library books he takes out of the house, because Mama and Daddy have enough to keep up with. We post a "Check yourselves" chalkboard by our front door, and one of the boys will call out the reminder before we leave so everyone will know to gather their drinks, shoes, wallets or anything else they might want to take with them.

Sometimes they forget, like the recent library book our oldest left at a playground overnight on a night when it rained, and then they learn the consequences of neglecting responsibility (he used a whole month's allowance and worked for the rest of the $30 fee by doing extra chores). Sometimes the consequence comes in the drinking from a public water fountain instead of a Thermos, or wearing the flip flops in the car instead of the tennis shoes he wanted but forgot to grab before he walked out the door.

5. Help is a way we love.

Most days we walk through our hours without enough hands, which means boys set the table and help wash dishes and sweep floors (Disclaimer: This is not to say we never have battles over chores or responsibilities. If you swing by our house every evening before and after dinner, you will hear a constant chorus of "I feel sick" and "I'm too tired" and "I hurt my arm on the playground today. I don't think I can pick up that fork."). They fetch diapers and close doors so twins can't destroy another room and clean up messes they may or may not have made. They help each other put on shoes and read to each other and grab the drink someone forgot. Sometimes they even keep twins out of things when Mama needs a bathroom break. Or a scream break. Or whatever.

We help, because we are a family, and this is what families do. These boys are learning compassion and care and kindness in the way they help.

This is not an exclusive list, by any means, just some of my favorites. Six kids is a trip, but I can say surely that I like the person I am today so much better than the one I used to be without them.

Kids have a transformational effect on their parents. I guess I just needed a little more work than most.

Dear Old Dad and Mom

The Perks of Being a Dad

Some men don't recognize the many perks of being a dad. They go about their day doing what they can (thank you, dads!) and being who they are and probably counting down the minutes until bedtime, just like moms are, because they know they have to get up tomorrow morning and do it all again.

There's nothing wrong with not noticing the perks of being a dad. But I thought it might be fun to point them out, in a spirit of celebration.

Husband gets to spend half his day hanging out with our six boys while I work, so he understands the perks of being a dad quite well. He knows that kids will always prefer their mamas (at least when they're young), but he has the opportunity to be a few things in their lives, too.

Namely:

1. A human jungle gym.

Husband likes to spread out on the floor and read books aloud or silently during our evening reading times. Every single time he does it, my boys climb on top of him. There are elbows and knees and chins everywhere. And I mean, literally, everywhere.

When he's standing still, they'll wrap their arms and legs around his feet and shins and "ride" to the dinner table. At bedtime they'll fight about who gets to climb on his back for the horse ride to their room. When he comes home from work they're already barreling toward him.

Not too long ago, when I fell down our stairs and broke my foot, Husband carried me out to the car so we could go get it X-rayed, since I was pretty sure, by the way my body wanted me to keep passing out, that it was broken (my body apparently does not have a fight or flight response to danger, only a shut down button). He injured his back in the process (you have to bend your knees, babe. I'm heavier than I look. You know, all that baby…muscle.)

When he saw the doctor about his back, the doctor told him it should be treated like any other injury. He should rest it. That night he stretched out on the floor to read a story (as if daring the powers that be), and one of the 3-year-olds did a cannonball onto his backside.

Good luck with the resting, dear. That back pain just might be around forever. Small price to pay, though. At least you still have your bladder function.

2. The yes man.

My kids go to their daddy when they want a yes.

"May I use the scissors to cut this paper into tiny little pieces you'll never be able to clean up?" they ask. (Not really. They really only ask for the scissors. But a mom always knows what that means.)

"Yes, as long as you clean it up," he says.

Yeah, right.

Our twins have bladders the size of walnuts. We remind them to go potty before we sit down to dinner, because if there's one thing I hate (there are more, I promise), it's interrupting dinner with a bathroom break. In my house, once someone mentions "potty," everyone suddenly remembers that they have to go, too. So it's important that they take care of this little inconvenience *before* they sit down at the table. And yet, inevitably, after they've used the potty and have been strapped in their booster seats for all of three bites, this is what happens:

Twin 1: I need to go potty.

Me: You just did.

Twin 1: I need to go again.

Twin 2: Yeah. Me too.

Me: Of course you do.

After this annoying exchange, I'll usually say something like "I'm sorry. You'll have to wait until after dinner," because the time it takes my boys to inhale their food is only about sixteen minutes, if we're lucky. If we're really lucky and we're having pizza, it's about seventeen minutes, because they just keep inhaling until it's gone.

And then one or the other twin will say, "I not talking to you. I talking to Daddy." Because, apparently, they've caught on to the fact that Husband doesn't really pay attention to conversations like the one above.

(This is changing. Husband's response now is "What did Mama say?" No more yes man, twins. Sorry you don't get to go potty three minutes after you already went.)

3. The I-don't-care man.

Husband takes things in so much better stride than I do.

"I used all the computer paper," the 8-year-old says. "But look at all these paper airplanes I made." (One hundred of them.)

"Wow," Husband says. "That's a lot of airplanes." Where I might have said: "Well, you're going to buy us a new package of computer paper, because I need that paper to print the second draft of my book in a couple of months."

I will cry over spilled milk and gripe about dinners wasted and stress about the lost library book, because we just paid for a lost book last week, and we can't keep doing this, it's going to break us, we won't be able to FEED THE KIDS SOON BECAUSE OF THE LOST LIBRARY BOOKS. But Husband just lets it roll right off. It's a little maddening. And also refreshing.

4. The Rule Relaxer.

Once a month I get together with a group of ladies to discuss life and work and the book we're supposed to read that month (but don't always get around to). This is Daddy's time to shine.

When I come home from these book club nights, at least two of my boys are passed out in the home library, where they've been reading since he "put them to bed," one is still working on a picture book in his bedroom with the light on, and two others are sleeping nearly on top of each other on the floor, in a massive pile of blankets, trying to get closest to the sliver of light streaming through their door.

On the mornings he watches them, they know they'll get blueberry muffins with real sugar instead of honey or pancakes with extra butter or a lunch that doesn't have any vegetables. It's like an surprise vacation for them.

5. The Life Speaker.

Dads have this amazing ability to be a life-speaker in the worlds of their children. Husband does this well.

When the 3-year-old stood up in his chair for the six billionth time during the same five-minute stretch of dinner (and I wished, for the six billionth time, that I had my voice recorded so all I had to do was press a button to hear, "Sit down on your bottom"), it didn't take him long to execute an epic fall, his legs and head facing straight up and his body caving toward the floor in the perfect pilates V-up (if a little crooked).

My first thought, on seeing him, was, "If you had been sitting in your chair like I told you, that wouldn't have happened." But the only thing Husband did was comfort him. He acknowledged how much it hurt to fall out of a chair you're standing in. And then he brought the lesson home.

A much better way to discipline, I think.

When Daddy is on duty, my boys get to watch more television, eat popcorn for lunch and change their clothes as many times as they want. I used to hate all these seemingly huge inconsistencies until I remembered how fortunate they are to have a loving dad in their life. So many kids don't.

My boys will never be the same because of their daddy. Their lives are richer for his presence and care.

I'm so very thankful he recognized the perks of being a dad.

Children Love in Invisible Ways

Every morning when I get him up to eat and every night before I put him to bed, I tell my 11-week-old that I love him.

I say it over and over and over, knowing that one day he will say those magical, heart-effectively-exploded words back to me. It's one of the best parts of being a mother—hearing that baby voice coo in a way that is surely "I love you," listening to the toddler echo, treasuring the spontaneous words from big-kid lips.

My boys rarely go a day without saying they love me, mostly because I can't go more than a few hours without telling them, and they can't just ignore me every time.

But even if they didn't tell me in words, I would know in a million other ways.

Sometimes, when we are wading through a week and there's just not enough time to get everything done and we've barely had a chance to sit down and talk about anything important, when we start feeling more like a maid and a shoe-finder and a diaper-changer and a laundry-doer and a cook and a story-reader and a do-your-homework-nagger and a get-back-in-bed-dang-it-yeller and an invisible piece in the world of partner and children, it can feel difficult to remember that we are loved and appreciated.

Our children, every moment, are loving us in a thousand different ways. Just like we show love in the little things—sorting socks and applying dish soap to that stubborn stain on his favorite shirt and keeping those art treasures in a hidden closet box—they are showing love in the little things, too.

Love doesn't always need words. It just needs eyes.

There is love in those shorts left on the floor—but not underwear, because he knows you hate it when he comes to dinner with a naked lower half.

There is love in those crayons spread all over the floor, because he was coloring a picture for you.

There is love in the "I hate you" he throws out so recklessly when you say it's no longer time to play with LEGOs, because he trusts you enough to share how he feels instead of locking those emotions tight.

There is love in his picking that first bloom on the peace lily that hasn't flowered since kids came along, because he wanted to give it to you.

There is love in that twelfth knock on your bedroom door after lights are out and they should be sleeping, because he spent all day at school and just can't get enough of his time with you.

There is love in the hug he gives you in the middle of the second- and third-grade hallway, because he didn't have to do it in front of all his friends—but he did.

There is love in pulling the dishwasher open and accidentally dumping out all the silverware, even though you've told him a billion times not to touch the dishes—he just wanted to help you.

There is love in the stuffing all his clean clothes into his underwear drawer, because he knows you like him to keep a tidy room.

There is love in the way they get up at 6 a.m. on the weekend and you have to drag them out of bed at 6:30 on the weekdays—because they know one means they have all day with you and the other means all day apart.

There is love in the note slid under the door, the one that says you're the meanest mama ever, because he feels safe enough in this home to express himself.

There is love in those forty cups lined up on the counter, waiting for washing, because they knew you wouldn't want them to drink from an already-dirty cup. Germs and all.

There is love in the egg smashed all over the floor, because he was just trying to bring you breakfast.

There is love in that unexpected mural on the wall, because he wanted to make you something beautiful, and this bare white wall looked like exactly the right place to do it.

There is love in the stuffed animal left in your room after fifteen reminders to get it, because he doesn't want you to be lonely.

There is love in his asking you to carry him downstairs, even though he has perfectly capable legs, because, deep down, he misses those mornings when you would do this all the time.

There is love in the running away, because he knows you care enough to chase him down, which you will. In your pajamas. With your partner's flip flops on, because it's all you could find.

There is love in the toddler attachment weighing down your leg while you're trying to take laundry out of the dryer, because he really just wants a two-arm hug. PUT THAT LAUNDRY DOWN, MAMA.

There is love in the interruptions that somehow find their way past a locked door, because you're his favorite person in the world (even though he's not really yours right this minute).

There is love in all the carpet stains and all the broken dishes and all the scratches on the walls—because they mean children felt comfortable enough in your home to really live.

This is how children love a mama.

This is Why My Kids Don't Have Any Friends

I'm the reason my kids don't have any friends.

That's not true, really. My kids have friends. They play with them at recess and collaborate with them in their classrooms and talk to them during P.E. when they're supposed to be doing six hundred jumping jacks. They just don't do much outside of school.

We have avoided play dates for eight years, but no longer.

On a recent day, a note came home from school with my 5-year-old, from the parents of a boy named Aaron* (*I've changed the name for privacy). My son had talked about this Aaron, so I knew they were good friends.

"Aaron would like to arrange a play date with your son," the note said.

I had no idea how to go about this.

The note, fortunately, listed telephone numbers and e-mail addresses for Aaron's mom and dad, asking me to "get in touch." Being the introverted person I am, I chose to text the numbers given. Surely that would be the easiest and definitely much less awkward than trying to fumble through a conversation on the phone with people I don't know.

Two days passed, and I heard nothing. That's when I assumed maybe the numbers given weren't cell phone numbers and didn't have text capacity. So I did the next best thing.

I e-mailed.

Meanwhile, I mentioned to my oldest son, who is 8, that his little brother was going to have a play date with a classmate and did he have anyone he would want to invite over for a play date, too? He had to think about this.

While he was thinking about it, my 5-year-old had his friend over, and it went well, and I was preoccupied wondering about the after-playdate etiquette—thank you note for letting him come over? Follow up of some kind? Reciprocated play date?—when my 8-year-old, one day after school, grabbed my hand and pulled me over to a woman I had never met, but clearly needed to, right this minute.

He didn't say a word of introduction.

We stared awkwardly at one another for a minute-that-felt-like-an-hour, before she held out her hand and said her name, which I didn't hear because my heart was roaring in my ears.

Awkward, awkward, awkward, it beat.

"I'm Christopher's* mom," she said. "He wanted to schedule a play date with J.M." (That's not really my son's name, of course. Maybe it's his initials. Maybe not.)

Oh no, oh no, oh no, not like this, not here, not in person. I wasn't expecting this. I wasn't prepared. I DON'T KNOW HOW TO DO THIS!

"Okay," I said, and then I realized I had no idea what to do next. I panicked a little and started babbling words that probably sounded something like this: "I don't have my phone or a piece of paper or a pen or anything at all to write with or record your number but do you have a phone or a piece of paper or a pen or anything at all to write with or record because if you do I could give you my number and then you could text me so I have yours and then we could figure out this playdate thing like when and where and how."

[Breathe.]

She looked at me like she'd been hit in the face by a spray of bullets. Which she had. Word bullets.

Aw, man, I thought. *My mouth and its word vomit just lost my boy a friend.*

"Oh. Oh, okay," she said, and I knew then, for sure, that I was doing this exactly wrong and weird and much more complicated than it needed to be done. Most people just pick a day, I'm sure. They set a time. It's easy. Except I was totally unprepared and didn't have my calendar with me and needed to talk to Husband…

She fumbled around in her pocket for her phone, trying to maintain her grip on the arm of her 2-year-old, who was trying to escape exactly like my 2-year-olds would have tried to escape, and I thought about how I would have felt the teensiest bit annoyed that the person talking to me couldn't see the struggle I was having, and couldn't we do this later?

Fail.

I started working on an apology to my son, because I knew his friend would never be allowed over to our house.

Christopher's mom took down my number, and my boys and I went home, and two days passed. Two days.

Then she texted, instead of calling, and invited my boy over. He and his friend played LEGOS for three hours, and when they were done, I walked to pick him up, and Christopher's mom invited me in, and we sat in clumsy conversation on her couch while our boys kept playing some more.

And that's when I realized she was just like me.

Awkward. Weird. Unpracticed at this whole playdate thing. (She was just like me!)

Her boy and mine have had another playdate since. And I might have made a new friend, too.

What My Baby Daddy Has Taught Me About Being a Parent

This year Husband shared a birthday with Mother's Day.

He's been just the tiniest bit overlooked for most of our parenting life because his birthday falls so close to Mother's Day, and all these boys in our house would much rather celebrate Mama than Daddy, at least for now.

So I didn't want the week to go by without expressing just what he's meant in my life and the life of my children.

When we were 18 and 19, Husband traveled to my hometown with me, because we were in a band together and were booked to play a concert. He stayed with some of my mom's friends.

"You'll marry that man," my mom's friend told me on the last day.

It was before I was even interested in him THAT way, so I shook my head. "No way," I said. "We're just friends. He's kind of a dork." (I was picky at 19.)

My mom's friend shrugged. "Okay," she said. "But you're going to marry him. Want to know how I know?"

Of course I wanted to know how someone knew who my future husband would be.

"Because of that," she said.

She pointed at him, sitting in the middle of a circle of children. They were all giggling hysterically, and when he stood up, they followed him like the Pied Piper (except less dangerously creepy.).

Three years later, I did marry him.

In the eight years we have parented our boys, I have watched him grow into one of the best fathers I've ever known. He has taught me better ways to love my children just because of the example he is.

Not only that, but he has taught me how to be a better parent, because it all comes so naturally to him.

He has taught me

1. Giggles are never too costly. He will do anything in the world to elicit giggles from his children. He will try to break dance on the carpet, tripping over his own feet. He will bound around the room on his hands and feet like a Daddy gorilla. He will read stories with their names replacing the words ("Shaggy dog, waggy dog, don't-do-as-you're Jadon dog."). He will trip himself on purpose or run into a wall or pretend he's slapping himself. He will turn them upside down to walk on the ceiling or body slam them on the couch or ask about their feelings in a robot voice. There is never a price too high.

2. There's no such thing as an embarrassed parent. When his son picked *Treasure Island* as his birthday party theme, Husband borrowed a pirate costume from his brother and stole my black eyeliner to rim his own eyes and read *A Pirate's ABC* with a roughened-sailor accent to all the kids gathered in our living room. When one son started dancing in the middle of the grocery store, because his jam came on over the loudspeaker, Husband joined him in a silly little dance of his own. When another son melted on the mulch of the neighborhood playground because he wasn't ready to go home yet, Husband bent beside him and acknowledged his feelings and the time and what he was expected to do next, instead of walking away and pretending that child wasn't his (which is exactly what I did).

3. Stories are much more fun when there are accents. Husband reads to his boys every night before they go to bed, and it's not unusual for me to hear an Englishman reading *Imagine a Day* or a Spanish man reading *Skippyjon Jones* or a dopey man reading *The Book With No Pictures.* When we're reading Elephant and Piggie books, he has voices for all the characters. He uses his hands. He makes it a show. He says I'm the reason they love to read, but the truth is, he has made books come alive for them. They love reading because of his theatrics.

4. Play is so much better than work. Husband has passed over good jobs because he wouldn't be home in time for family dinner. He has turned down promotions. He has limited work-from-home hours because he wants to protect family play time after dinner, when he'll run around the cul-de-sac playing kickball or trying to get a kite in the air or chasing all the kids for an epic game of tag or (our favorite) playing dodgeball. When it's raining, he pulls out Jenga and Monopoly and Battleship or makes up his own game of charades. His boys know their relationship is more important than what work their daddy might have to get done at night.

5. Kids are not too young to add value to the world. So many kids feel like they have nothing to offer the world, but Husband lets our boys know they do. He encourages their creativity. He makes up secret codes with them. He designs the book covers for the books they've written. He lets them use all the computer paper to make paper airplanes they'll sell in their art stand out front. He writes silly songs with them. He outlines that hand-lettering piece he drew and lets them color it in. He teaches them, and he lets himself be taught by them. He believes in them, and he teaches them to believe in themselves.

The other day, we were leaving a meeting when all five of the potty-trained boys announced that they needed to go potty. I rolled my eyes, because it happens EVERY time, but Husband laughed and raced them out of the car.

They walked up some wooden stairs, the boys behind him and all around him, and I saw the same picture I'd seen fourteen years ago, all these kids gathered around him just because they love being around a man like him. I couldn't help but smile—because it's plain to see the love he has for them and the love they have for him and the rock of a relationship that has been building since they slid into his life.

How fortunate I am that my boys have a daddy like him.

A Mother is a Warrior Who Never Goes Off Duty

No one ever told me how hard this would be.

I took that first pregnancy test while Husband was away at work, and I nearly passed out with the fear of it. But then I told him, and we cried, and then we told our family, and it was only congratulations and cheers and excitement at this new chapter of our lives. And no one ever said that "a mother continues to labor long after the baby is born" (Lisa-Jo Baker, *Surprised by Motherhood*).

And then we brought him home in the backseat of our car, where I sat while Husband drove 30 miles per hour below the speed limit down a busy highway, and we got to the home that was now his home and he cried in the arms of his grandmother, my mother, and she handed him back to me as if I knew what to do with him, and it was then that I realized it would always be me.

I was the one he'd come to with an empty cup for the milk-refilling, and I was the one he'd need to sharpen the pencil he was using to write his story, and I was the one who could magically kiss away the hurt when he stubbed his dirty toe on the sidewalk lip.

I was it. I was all. I was Mama.

And maybe it didn't fully sink in, the knowing that I would never have a day off, until that day I got sick or that day I felt too tired to be a mother or that day I needed to work a few extra hours.

I was barely able to climb out of bed one morning, but I was not allowed to call in sick to mothering. I had stayed awake all night with the newest baby, but I was not allowed to hold up my "just too tired" sign the next morning when the oldest crashed into my room before the sun had even woken. I put that "working" door hanger on my door while their daddy was on duty, and it would not stop them from barging in to ask me if I could help them get dressed so they could go out front and ride their scooters.

A mother is a warrior who never goes off duty.

These babies grow inside us, connected to our life source so our heart pumps their growing with every beat, and they develop fully and completely and beautifully, and then we bear down and push them out into the world, and even though the doctors cut that cord, severing the physical connection, they are still attached to our hearts in every way invisible, by heartstrings that let out slack when we'd like them to give us space and then pull back in when we need them close.

And sometimes we want to let out that slack but they're not quite ready to take it, so we feel suffocated and used up and empty, and we wonder when they will ever, ever, ever do this one thing, just this one thing, just this tying a shoe, just this pouring their own milk, just this washing their own body during bath time. And sometimes they need that slack but we don't want to give it, because he is our baby and we are his mama, and look how long those legs grew overnight and look at that face without the squishy spot above the eyebrows and look at those hands that tie shoes and pour milk and bathe all on their own.

Every loosen and pull of those heart-strings is like a squeezing of our hearts, because, yeah, it's a thankless job, and, yeah, the days feel never-ending, and, yeah, sometimes we wonder why we did it in the first place or had so many so close or chose large family over small, but we wear that name, Mama, Mother, Mom, with great pride and hope and most of all love. It's harder than hard, this mothering, and some days we love it and some days we don't.

Seize the moment is really the only possible mantra for a mama.

Because there are days when he's dumped out his milk every time our back was turned so he could smear it onto all those spots we just cleaned thirteen seconds ago, and there are days when the yelling moments have outnumbered the not-yelling moments, and there are days we really like our kids and there are days we wish we could give them away. But tucked between the frustrations of those days are the moments that make us glad, that tell us we wouldn't change a thing, that shout it all over the hard, hard, hard places: "I am a mother, and there is nothing so outrageously challenging and outrageously beautiful in all the world."

And it's true. There isn't.

These moments we seize are the gift of our lives, mamas. They help us carry on. They are light in the dark places.

So seize the moment, warrior mama. And let it be the gift of your life.

Grinding Through the Day to Day

Cinder-Mama is a Real Person. She is Me.

You know that scene in Cinderella where she's in the kitchen trying to get things ready for the day, and on the wall there's this collection of bells ringing incessantly, signaling that people who are depending on her (mostly because they're lazy) need things? Every morning, my kitchen fills with its own chorus of little bells, too, except those bells are walking around in the form of two 3-year-olds, a 5-year-old, a 6-year-old and an 8-year-old, and I can't just simply leave the room to get away from their clanging, because they have legs and will follow me to the edge of the world without asking any questions about where I'm going.

"Mama!" the 5-year-old will say in the whiniest voice I've ever heard (and that's saying a lot. I've really cleaned up my act.). "I can't find my shoes."

He's not even out of bed yet, so I'm pretty sure he hasn't even attempted "looking," which I put in quotations because "looking" for a 5-year-old consists of sometimes seeing what's right in front of his face, sometimes not. He just tripped over one of those missing shoes, and he still hasn't found them.

His bell is followed up closely by one of the twins saying, "Mama, my brudder beat me down the stairs." If only I could turn back time. Followed, almost in the same breath, by his twin brother saying, "Mama, I firsty. I need milk, Mama. Mama, I need milk. I firsty, Mama" without even the slightest pause so that I can let him know that his milk is already on the table if he would just "look."

"Where's my blue folder?" the 8-year-old will say, even though I'm not the one in charge of his blue folder and there's a designated place for it and I can see it sticking out from that designated place right this very minute.

"Oh! I forgot (fill in the blank)," the 6-year-old says on a regular basis. Usually that fill-in-the-blank looks something like forgetting that he's VIP student this week and he needs to bring a poster with pictures of himself and his family on it so that all the other students will know who he is and what he wants to be when he grows up. Or forgetting that he's supposed to have his book club book finished today, and he still has seventy-five pages to read. Or forgetting that there was a birthday party he was invited to this weekend, and he didn't get to go, and how can we possibly keep track of all this?

Get me a drink, I hungry, I can't find my shoes, where's my library book, please hold me just because, help me, carry me, push in my chair, where's my folder, sign my papers, I'm cold, I'm hot, I'm hungry, I need my vitamins, bring me my blanket, where's my backpack, can you turn on the light, I need more toilet paper, I want more, More, MORE.

With all these children and all their constant demands, sometimes I start feeling a little like Cinderella. Cinder-Mama, to be more accurate. It's like the fairy tale I always wanted, except it's not.

Brush my hair, wash me off, wipe my bottom, what's ten plus ten, I want my color book, the baby's getting into the crayons, button my pants, tie my shoes, help me up, kiss this hurt, when's dinner, can we go to the store because I have two dollars to spend, I need a snack, I can't open the toothpaste, aw, man, it's the minty toothpaste, I like the strawberry toothpaste, what are you doing? Going to the bathroom? You don't have a penis, where does your peepee come out?

There is something inherent in a mama that hears a need and wants to meet it, desperately, right this minute. But the thing is, if I try to meet every single need in my house, I will go a little crazy.

Because one minute the 5-year-old will need someone to show him how to tie his shoes, again, and, at the same time, the 6-year-old will want help pouring the milk, because it's a new gallon and I'm really thankful that he's asking because the last thing I want is a whole gallon of milk dumped out onto the floor, but there's no way in the world that I can be in two places at one time, so one of those needs is going to have to remain unmet until I can manage it or he learns how to do it himself.

I tried to be in two places at once one time, and I ended up feeling resentful and angry that they would ask me to do so many things at the same time even though there was only one of me and six of them. So I had to take a step back. I had to breathe. I had to say it was okay that I couldn't meet every single need the first time they asked. Or even the fifth time they asked. Or ever, sometimes (they did, after all, wish they could have gone to that party they missed. I was Cinder-Mama, not Fairy GodMama). It was good for them to learn how to wait. It was good for them to learn to do things for themselves. It was good for them to realize they were fully capable of doing what I could do.

So they started tying their own shoes, because they figured out they could do hard things. They started pouring their own milk, even if it was a brand new gallon, because they knew they had permission to screw up and spill, as long as they cleaned it up. They started writing their own events on a calendar and waiting to be hugged and kissed and taking responsibility for their backpacks and shoes and school folders.

They don't always remember, of course. There are mornings when it still sounds like there are shrieking bells wrapped around my ankles. There are days they forget "mama" is not synonymous with "servant," but they are learning, day by day by day, that they are fully capable of handling the world on their own.

No more Cinder-Mama. Except for my indescribable beauty, of course.

My Kids Know and Use the Worst F-Word of Them All

My boys are playing together just fine over in a corner of the dining room, on the glass table we never use for eating, (because it's glass and kids have twelve thousand fingers). They're occupied with LEGOs, building a Fun Land with slides and computers and a playground, so it looks like the perfect opportunity to sneak into the kitchen and cram down another of those dark chocolate brownies I made last night, even though I just got done telling them, when they asked, that it's too early in the morning to have one.

I should know better by now. I mean, I've been a parent for eight years. I should know that in a household of kids, there is never, ever, ever a perfect opportunity. But sometimes I go a little wild and get my hopes up.

So I'm in the middle of cramming, hiding in the pantry just in case they come wandering into the kitchen, when the 8-year-old catches me, red-handed, with chocolate all over my fingers (the curse of gooey brownies).

He looks from my face to my hands and back again. And then he tosses out that bad word I just love to hate: "Aw, no f**r. You ate a brownie. You said it was too early for us to have one."

I think fast. "Well," I say. "I'm a grownup. When you're a grownup you get to eat whatever you want in the morning."

Real smooth, I know. A GREAT example of the way I DON'T

want my children to eat. Well, parenting and paradoxes go hand in hand.

Hours later, when it's time for lunch, I pile some strawberries and sliced cucumber on their plates beside their PB&J sandwiches. Off to the side, I put a handful of raisins on everyone's plate except the 8-year-old, who doesn't like raisins. I give him pecans.

His brothers notice, of course. "No f**r," the 5-year-old says. "He gets pecans."

"You have raisins," I say. "He doesn't like raisins. I'll take your raisins and give you pecans, if you want."

He shuts his mouth and shakes his head, because, of course, he prefers the sweet raisins to the pecans.

I get so tired of the F word, typically used in the phrase "No f**r." My boys are creative, so they have several variations. They might say "It's not f**r" or "That's not f**r" or "You should be f**r" and so many more iterations I can't even remember all of them right now, in my annoyed, flustered, I'm-so-sick-of-this state of mind. All I know is I hear them 15 billion times a day.

When someone goes out to play because he's finished his after dinner chore: "That's not f**r. He gets to go play already, and I'm still stuck here doing dishes." When someone pours his own milk and it's half a centimeter more than I gave his brother: "It's not f**r. He got more milk than I did." When someone comes down the stairs with a red shirt on: "No f**r. I never get to wear a red shirt."

What I want to say every single time I hear these delightful words is, "Welp. Life's not f**r. The sooner you can learn that and accept it, the better."

What I usually do, instead, because I'm a good parent, is

empathize with their feelings and then explain exactly why fair isn't equal. Sometimes they understand. Most times they don't.

But I'd be lying if I said it didn't take incredible strength of will to keep calm when they're throwing out and kicking around the f-word. In fact, this is what it usually sounds like in my head:

When we're eating dinner, and their daddy and I have a glass of wine:

3-year-old: "No f**r. You get wine."

What I want to say: "If you only knew who I'd be without it…"

What I say instead: "Want to taste?"

He gets close enough to smell and picks up his cup of milk without a single complaint.

That's right, son. This stuff is NASTY, because it's cheap and it's survival.

When we're watching a movie and the boys get their cups of popcorn:

6-year-old: "Hey, no f**r! He got more than I did!"

What I want to say: "Wow. Aren't you an efficient counter? You know fractions already? Because he has half a kernel more than you."

What I say instead: "Here. Have another."

Because, dang, I don't want this fight. I know what it will look like. It will look like five cups of popcorn dumped onto the floor so they can count it, and the 3-year-olds can't even count past twelve, which means this will take ALL DAY.

When the older boys are sitting around during art time, and the 8-year-old decides he's going to make the most epic paper airplane ever.

5-year-old: "No f**r. He knows how to make a paper airplane."

What I want to say: "Stinks to be you."

What I say instead: "Here. Let's learn how to make one."

Forty minutes later we have a paper airplane that won't even fly, because making paper airplanes is much more complicated than it looks.

When it's almost nap time, and I'm telling the 3-year-old twins what they need to do next.

3-year-old: "No f**r. My bruvers get to have Quiet Time and I have to take a nap."

What I want to say: "Only boys who know how to properly say the word 'brothers' get to have Quiet Time. Besides, I don't need a break from your brothers. You, on the other hand…I need a thousand-day break from you."

What I say instead: "Do you want to crawl like a dog to your bed or run like an ostrich?"

During dinner, the oldest is sitting beside his littlest brother, watching me feed him.

8-year-old: "No f**r. You get to feed him."

What I want to say: "What the—?"

What I say instead: "You can do it if you want."

Two minutes later, the baby sneezed sweet potatoes all over his oldest brother's face, and I had to bite my lip to keep from laughing hysterically. Not so fun now, is it?

Everybody in my house knows this bad word. Everyone uses it. We're born knowing how to use it, I think.

Kids have such a messed up definition of what f**r really is. Unfortunately, that doesn't make the feeling of unf**r any less real to them.

The other day, when we were playing a game and one of his brothers drew a yellow card he needed, my 6-year-old said, "That's not f**r."

"What does f**r mean?" I said.

No one answered, because none of them knows. All they know is they want life to work for them right now. They want it to be perfectly smooth and perfectly easy and perfectly their way.

And, honestly, so do I. But I've been alive longer than they have, and I know it's just not. I know it's not f**r that some lose babies while others get to keep them. I know it's not f**r that some business deals fall through and we suddenly can't make our mortgage payment this month. I know it's not f**r that the store was out of raw oats so now I have to think outside the box for Wednesday morning's breakfast.

So much about life is not f**r. So many times I want to stomp and complain and throw out those same words my kids overuse. Because it's not f**r that my air conditioner broke and we had to try to sleep through four days of 1,000-degree heat. It's not f**r that my kids don't listen to what I'm saying 99.7 percent of the time because they have better things on their minds. It's not f**r that last night, when I had just slipped into dreamland, one of them came knocking on my door to say he couldn't sleep, and then it took me three hours to get back to sleep so I'm more exhausted than normal today.

In a child's life, f**r means get-what-I-want. Everything they want to be f**r—a game, the ability to make epic paper airplanes, a treatment—is strictly for their own benefit. They want a f**r game, because they want to win. They want a f**r ability, because it means they wouldn't have to ask Mama's help and their paper airplane would actually fly. They want f**r treatment, because they're afraid they're missing out on something special.

We're born with this complex. We all know adults who still have trouble accepting its reality in their lives. That, to me, means it's good for our kids to practice surviving "unf**r," because they get to learn, in the process, that life doesn't end because something doesn't go exactly the way they planned or even hoped.

That's what develops grit.

So, today, when the 8-year-old plops on the couch and says, "I want to watch a movie," and I answer in the negative, and he says, "It's not f**r. My friends get to watch TV all day," and it's the sixtieth time I've heard those blasted words in an hour, I send them all outside to jump out their frustration on the trampoline. And when the last one gets out the door, I turn the lock. No one's coming back inside until dinner.

Life isn't f**r, after all.

The Daily Overstimulation Cycle of an Introverted Mom

I am a highly sensitive introvert living in the middle of a crowd.

Here is what my daily overstimulation cycle looks like:

Boy #1 wakes in a bad mood because he stayed up too late trying to finish a book he was reading, and now his foul mood has followed him down the stairs and to the table, where it sits between his brothers and his mad-scientist hair spearing that crumpled-with-grouch brow.

Boy #3 must be carried downstairs because his legs don't work in the morning.

Boy #4 and Boy #5 wait for the carry downstairs for breakfast because if I set them loose, they'll never find their way down but, instead, will pull every book from the shelves in our library before I've even finished changing out of my pajamas.

Boy #3 says he really wanted the blue plate instead of the green one that sits before him.

Boy #2 interrupts the morning devotional to say I forgot to give them milk.

Boy #1 races up the stairs, grazing me on the way up so he can pick out clothes and then forget to put them on because he discovered he forgot to hang up one very important poster on his wall that needs to be hung up right this very minute.

Boy #3 needs me to get him some underwear out of his child-locked drawer because he slept without any last night.

Boy #2 squeezes the toothpaste while trying to open it because his toothbrush, which I already swiped with toothpaste, fell on the floor and now it's dirty, and his squeezing makes a sticky mess all over the counter, but don't worry, he'll clean it up, and he does. With his tongue.

Boy #1 gets the first of a thousand reminders that he needs to get dressed and brush his teeth.

Boy #3 needs me to help him put on his shoes.

Boy #2 skips from the tongue-cleaned-countertops bathroom into the room he shares with his brother so he can more efficiently distract him at closer proximity.

Boy #3 is now whining that he can't find his shoes, much less put them on.

Boy #1 is telling me about a dream he had last night while I pick out clothes for Boy #4 and Boy #5, while Boy #2 is telling me I forgot to give them a piece of their Halloween candy at lunch yesterday and they should get double today, and Boy #3 is saying something about how no one will help him, but I can't really hear his complaints over all the other noise.

Boy #3 is yelling that Boy #5 is climbing out of his seat and sitting on his high chair tray.

Boy #4 is screaming because he can't figure out how to do the same.

Boy #3 is saying something like we'll never, ever, ever find his shoes, while Boy #2 is reminding me that I forgot to give him his melatonin last night and why didn't I give it to him and what if I never give it to him ever again, and Boy #1 is asking why can't he wear sweat pants to school like all the other boys in his class.

Boy #1 gets his thousandth warning, and I race Boy #2 down the stairs so we can find Boy #3's shoes and get Boys #4 and 5 dressed and head out the door, even if Boy #1 is still not ready.

Boy #4 is dressed and straining against me while I buckle him into his stroller, screaming at the lockdown.

Boy #5 fights the dressing because he observed what just happened to his brother, and he strains against me while I buckle him into his stroller, and he, too, screams at the lockdown.

Boy #1 is begging me to help him with his shoes because he still doesn't know how (or, more likely, have the energy) to tie them, and Boy #2 is talking about how I forgot to let them play outside last night, and Boy #3 is lying on the floor whining because he still hasn't found the shoes that are caressing his cheek.

Boy #1 must be reminded to get his backpack on the way out the door, and just before I lock the door because we're finally ready to go, ten minutes late, Boy #2 says I forgot to get him a jacket and I also didn't give them all their vitamins today and I just have to give them their vitamins before they go to school because what if I forget again.

Boy #2 races ahead on a scooter, waving at all the high school students we pass on our walk, and Boy #1 rides his scooter just beside the stroller wheels because he wants to tell me about this new science experiment he's going to try when he gets back home today, and Boy #3 falls behind, whining that he cannot go fast up the hill.

Boy #3 whines that we're leaving him behind because he's not moving at all, and he makes a little effort to catch up and then whines that he just can't do it, see? and I take a deep breath and just keep moving.

It's only 7:25 a.m. and I'm already exhausted.

After reading Susan Cain's book, *Quiet: The Power of Introverts in a World That Can't Stop Talking*, I learned much about the introvert's stimulation cycle; about how overstimulation can leave one feeling fatigued and irritable and anxious, and how this is perfectly normal; about the importance of recharging with quiet solitude throughout the day.

Sometimes good parenting looks like taking a time out of our own, closing our bedroom door for just a minute's peace, sending children outside for the relief of alone, recognizing the need for space and freedom—because we are better people for it. Sometimes the work of self-compassion is the hardest work of all, when children must be dressed and vitamins must be parceled out and toothpaste must be wiped from sticky countertops.

Always, something else begs our attention. But the truth is, we can better approach the daily work of parenting only after we have rested ourselves. I know this. I suspect we all do.

So today, after clearing lunch away and tucking boys in beds and setting aside all those other responsibilities that lengthen my to-do list for a later time, I close my door and turn the lock without the usual separation guilt, and I find my center again in the calm expanse of solitude.

Sweet, sweet solitude.

Now I can breathe.

What Happens When a Kid Environmentalist is on Trash Duty

We have this fancy chalkboard hanging in our kitchen with "This Night" written in wannabe hand lettering, because I'm nothing more than a wannabe artist. Beneath those words, we have each of the boys' names and their subsequent chores listed. Those chores change every week, although if you ask our boys, they're always on wipe-the-table duty, because it only takes thirty seconds to flick a sponge around and dump food scraps on the floor.

We're diligent about teaching our boys how to do chores, because one day they will be married (if they so choose), and they need to know how to do things like sweep the floor and load a dishwasher (or whatever nifty invention is around then) and wipe down counters until they're squeaky clean (no, that's squeaky clean, kids. Not sticky clean.) so their significant other can take a little break every now and then. Also so we can get a break for the next eighteen years, but that's not really the point. Okay, it is.

Normally doing the chores looks like the 3-year-old putting the silverware in the dishwasher tray and pouring in the liquid soap and closing it and pressing start, but not getting to touch anything else (because glass in 3-year-old hands is like a death sentence. Also, speaking of a death sentence, you should make sure there's not a butcher knife in the silverware tray, because even if it's already safe and snug in its place, a 3-year-old will pull it back out. "Not here,

Mama. Here," he'll say, waving it like he's writing the ABCs in the air. Except he doesn't know how to write letters yet. So he's really just passive-aggressively threatening you for all those times you took the plunger away from him even though it's his favorite toy that's most definitely not a toy.).

"Doing chores" looks like the other 3-year-old singing while he's wiping down the table, which really just means he's sweeping all the leftover food (because boys eat like raccoons) onto the floor the 5-year-old is complaining about sweeping. It looks like a 6-year-old "wiping off counters" by maneuvering the sponge around all the papers they unloaded from their school folders and spread all over the available surface space so there's really nothing at all to wipe.

And then there is the 8-year-old on trash duty.

When this boy is on trash duty, I regret all the times I talked to him about environmental issues like saving water and recycling everything we can recycle and not wasting energy by leaving lights on. The only thing he heard was…nothing. He read in a book somewhere that most trash can be reused, and this is his mantra:

Everything can be reused.

(Because he likes absolutes.)

This mantra is a little overly simple, to my mind. I remind him of this every time he's brushing his teeth and walks out of the bathroom with the water faucet still running because he's thinking about how he could reuse his toothbrush and all his brothers' toothbrushes to make a little toothbrush family with drawn-on faces and homemade clothes and handmade arms and how about we get started right now. I remind him every time I run upstairs before we leave for school and four lights are blazing because he was trying to find that one book to show me what someone made out of old shoes. I remind him every time I throw something away and it ends up back on my bed.

Take, for instance, the baby's old pacifiers. Pacifiers are pretty gross. These things have been through five boys, and the last baby decided he didn't like them, so we thought we'd just toss all the old ones. I didn't really want to give them away because five boys and all that slobber—who in the world would want them? I tossed them all in my bathroom trash can and thought I was done with that.

Imagine my surprise when I wanted to go to bed and there were four pacifiers staring at me from my pillow.

"What in the world?" I said, to no one in particular.

"Oh. Those pacifiers can be reused," said the 8-year-old, who always seems to be behind me, even if it's time for lights out.

"I threw them away for a reason," I said. "I do not want to reuse your old pacifiers." I then explained that we didn't want to pass the old pacifiers along to another family when they had already been used by him and four of his brothers, because sometimes people can be a little weird about that kind of thing, since pacifiers go in boys' mouths and, if the twins have anything to say about it, other unmentionable places.

"Then I'll take them," he said. He held out his hand.

"I don't want old pacifiers all over the place. We're already fighting a losing battle with tidying up," I said, because I'm a positive person like that. "And we're not having any other babies."

"I know," my boy said. "But I can use them to make something."

And he did. He made a pacifier yo-yo that lasted all of three days before he got tired of playing with it.

When the environmentalist is on trash duty, we can't throw anything away. The leftover food scraps can always be used to feed the birds out back. The plastic strawberry cartons can be used to hold cloth napkins and keep random things organized (just get out of my house, random things. I don't even want you here.). The old socks with holes in them can be reused for cleaning cloths—except they're my infant's socks that the 3-year-olds cut holes in and are about as big as my thumb. I guess I can…clean the baseboards. With one finger. And an old infant sock.

I've come up to my room to find old makeup boxes and papers I no longer need and soap-scummed shampoo bottles lying on my bed because he thinks I can "find a way to reuse them if I just think hard enough." Problem is, I don't really have much of a brain left to think outside the box, because children are like zombies except way cuter, so you don't suspect that all they really want to do is eat your brain.

I know I should be glad he cares. But when you're slipping into bed and find an old pair of mangled underwear because he saw it in your trash can and decided you probably needed it and didn't really mean to throw it away, and you know exactly what the skivvies were touching in the trash, I think it's time to close up the environmentalist shop.

But the thing is, I don't want to squash that spirit. Because the way he can so clearly see something new out of something old is a great quality to have. It doesn't happen for all of us, and many of us lose that ability, anyway, when we become practical adults and too much stuff is a very real thing. Right now, he loves seeing what he can do to create something new and fun out of something old and worn. This is valuable experience he's getting with play and invention and creativity. I don't want to discourage that.

I also don't want to try to imagine what I could possibly do with my old Physician's Formula organic mascara tube that you'd never be able to clean out. Just get rid of it, son. Trust me. That thing will start smelling worse than your feet in six months.

So we've reached a compromise. As long as his reclaimed items have a place, he can keep them. As long I've put something in the trash, he's not allowed to put it back on my bed with his "imagine what else it could be" challenge.

It's working, for now. At least until the next time I throw away a pair of blown-out-soles shoes and he decides we can probably figure out a way to use all that rubber for something like a homemade Honda Odyssey tire. Which is just around the corner, I'm sure.

Why I Actually Dread Bedtime Right Now

It's been a month since I looked forward to bedtime.

Usually this time, 8 p.m. sharp, is a brilliant shining light in the long stretch of a boy-filled day, because it's the time I finally get to hide away in my room and ignore those non-emergency cries and hang out with my husband or read or just go to bed myself.

But we've been potty training twins, and now they're in a room they can escape from, because how can you successfully potty train a 2-year-old without giving them access to the potty at night?

Bedtime has now officially become drive-Mama-crazy time.

Because now it's not just the cries of older boys that come knocking on our door ("I need some pajamas" from the just-turned-8-year-old, who still hasn't put away last week's laundry, so his pajamas are buried beneath all those Star Wars books scattered all over his room; a "Where's my blanket?" from the 5-year-old, because earlier today someone, I don't know who—everybody has their own blankets and he says he didn't do it—carried it downstairs and decided it was too much work to bring it back up; and "I don't have a pillow" from the 4-year-old who doesn't look very well, because there's a pillow right beside his face. His cheek is touching it.)

Now the (maybe emergency? maybe not?) cries of twins have joined the cacophony.

"I need go poo poo in the potty bad, Mama," they say. (Do they?

I just don't know. Should I risk it? Probably not.)

"I pee pee in my underwear, Daddy," they say. (We check. It seems to be a threat of some kind.)

"I poo poo. Ew!" (This one brings a mama and daddy running, but it also seems to be an empty threat—at least until the day we decide to ignore it.)

Potty training is challenging, because it's so dang hard to know when they're telling the truth or just stalling bedtime. So, for a while, every time one of those calls came, we let them out of bed to go potty.

Here's what would happen 99 percent of time.

One twin: "I need go poo poo really bad, Mama."

Other twin: "Me too."

Mama: "OK. One at a time."

I take one twin out of the room to go potty, and on the way there he finds a stuffed frog he didn't even know he was missing until he saw it, so he picks it up. Then he sees a book he wants to put back on the library shelf and a toy that shouldn't even be upstairs and a piece of paper he wants to throw in the trash when he finally (if ever) makes it to the bathroom.

Mama: "Looks like you didn't have to go so badly after all."

Twin, shaking his head. "I go bad, Mama."

Mama: "Then let's go to the bathroom."

Twin: "OK."

Once on the potty, he'll strain for a few seconds, just to put on a show, and a little pee trickles out, probably so I can't say he didn't have to go, because look, he did, and then he says, "Done."

Repeat with twin 2.

I caught on to their little game.

So lately, when those cries start coming, we give them one more potty escapade, whatever it may look like, and then we tell them they need to hold it until morning, and we cross our fingers.

I've never been a big fan of transitions like these, because they can seem so difficult and never-ending when we're right in the middle of them, but we've had three other boys who prove that someday, maybe weeks from now or maybe (God forbid) months from today, these twins will know and understand the rules, and bedtime will become the sweet time it was meant to be for all parents everywhere in the world.

Transition times will always, eventually, someday, smooth into normalcy.

One of these days, our twins will realize that their I-need-to-potty cries aren't working anymore, because we just took them five minutes ago, and they couldn't possibly need to go again already, but for now, they'll play their little game and we'll keep wondering and hoping and crossing fingers.

For now, I will dread bedtime because it's no longer rest time. For now, I will sit in the library recliner instead of lying in my comfy bed, reading in between those reminders for twins to stay in their beds, reminding myself when I feel like crying that this won't last forever.

Thank God it won't last forever.

Hey, Kids: Don't Do It. A Mom Always Knows.

The other afternoon I was sitting in our library reading a book, because it has a direct line to my 3-year-old twins' room, and they're not traditionally great nappers.

I guess they didn't know I was watching, because one of them was hanging from his top bunk like a monkey, trying to swing into his brother's bottom bunk. The other was laughing hysterically.

"Get back in your bed," I said, startling him so much he lost his grip and crashed to the floor.

"You scared me," he shouted as he was climbing back up the steps to his bed.

I didn't feel sorry for him, though, because how many times have I told him not to hang off the side of the bed like that? At least twenty billion.

There is something I've noticed about my boys. When they think they can get away with something—not because they've gotten away with it before, ever, but because they think someone's just not paying attention—they will do it.

It's easy to understand in a house with so many kids and so few parent eyes, but there's something they haven't quite figured out.

This mom sees and knows everything.

So, in the interest of helping them out with this hard-to-understand mystery, I've compiled an easy-to-read list of everything a mom knows.

1. I know what you're doing, even if I can't see you.

Call it eyes on the back of my head, call it intuition, call it whatever you want. I know. I know that when you go to the bathroom, you are probably going to play with the plunger because you've done it six thousand times before. I know that when you go upstairs (and I know when you do), you will head straight for Daddy's forbidden computer and that your inexperienced fingers will close out PhotoShop, along with the latest project your daddy forgot to save, on your way to Cool Math.

I know that when you think you escaped unnoticed from the house, you will immediately run toward the neighbor's rock path you've been told not to touch. I know that when you disappear into the pantry, you are looking for the raisins, because they're still spilled on the floor from the last time you tried, unsuccessfully, to sneak a snack three minutes after you'd eaten your lunch—which included your weight in watermelon. I know that if you beat me to the library by half a second there will already be fifty books scattered on the floor that you'll try to hide by shoving them all under the couch.

I know.

2. I know you don't think I'm paying attention, but I am. Always.

When that phone call comes through and you think my attention is split, you should know that I'm still paying attention.

I know what you're doing on the stairs because I can hear the footfalls leading up to the baby gate you'll dismantle in three seconds. I know the sound of the closet door opening means you think you can sneak Battleship from its hiding place and dump out those red and white pieces without getting caught.

I know that because it seems like I'm paying full attention to the phone conversation and not at all to you, you will try to get a cup out of the dishwasher and fill it with water you'll spill three steps from the water dispenser, even though I gave you milk in your Thermos sixty seconds ago.

I know.

3. I know as soon as I leave the room you will think about doing what you've been told not to do.

I know that if I go upstairs to get your baby brother, you will try to take the lid off that LEGO container Daddy left on the counter so you can scatter the pieces into a land mine before I get back (and if you can't get the lid off you will destroy the container). I know that as soon as I go to the bathroom you will climb onto the table and steal that crayon you wanted from your brother. I know that as soon as I disappear to put your baby brother down for a nap you will open the refrigerator and try to stuff as many grapes as you can get into your mouth before I get back.

I know what's in your mouth and the toy you snuck up to your bed for some naptime fun and the thing you're thinking about right this minute.

4. I know quiet doesn't always (hardly ever?) mean good.

I know that sometimes it means you're coloring your carpet red with a crayon you found hidden in the cushions of the couch. I know it means you have unraveled the whole roll of eco-friendly paper towels because you wanted to make a paper bag for your cars. I know it means you're probably trying to fit into a shirt for a six-month-old, even though you're 3. Your quiet isn't fooling me at all.

I know all of this mostly because

5. I know you.

I know your adventurous spirit that catapults you out the door and halfway down the road before your daddy and I can even get out of the kitchen. I know your creativity that turns a door into a canvas. I know your curiosity that puts a cup with a car submerged in water into the freezer to see what happens.

I know your playful nature that sees everything—a plunger, a roll of paper towels, butter knives—like it's a new toy. I know how hard it is to tame the strong will that sees a challenge in every don't-do-it.

I know you, all the wild and all the crazy and all the most beautiful pieces, too.

And guess what? I love it all.

But next time you decide to see what happens when you put a balloon in the toilet and try to pee on it, just remember: You will be caught. I promise.

A mom always knows.

So don't even think about it.

How to Talk Like a 3-Year-Old

We've been working on manners in our house. This might seem like a losing battle with a bunch of boys who think it's hilarious to arm-fart while they're covering their mouth coughing, but nobody ever said I wasn't up for a challenge. I am the only female in a household of seven males, after all. Challenge accepted.

By far the rudest people in my house are my 3-year-old twins.

They make demands, no matter how many times we tell them we're not demand-givers. They brutally tell the truth ("Are you having another baby, Mama?" No, ~~little devil~~ sweet boy, that's just the after-pregnancy pooch. Seven months later.). They pick up words from their older brothers and try to use them in sentences that don't make sense ("I need very literally to the potty." What does that even mean, son?). They love the word NO, in all caps. They have their own opinions about what they think should happen, and it's not ever what you think should happen. Ever.

If you have the great privilege of living with or caring for a 3-year-old on a daily basis, you're probably very familiar with the following:

Me: Please put your shoes on. We need to take your brothers to school.

3-year-old: NO!

Me: Yes.

3-year-old: But I too tired.

Me: Okay. You can stay here and go to bed.

3-year-old: Actually I hungry.

Me: You just ate three eggs and a two pancakes. There's nothing left.

3-year-old: But I firsty.

Me: You can get a drink at the water fountain after we drop your brothers off.

3-year-old: But there are crayons on the floor.

Me: I'm getting tired of your buts.

3-year-old: Mama! You said butt!

Me: Just get your shoes on.

3-year-old: NO!

On and on and on it goes, until I'm carrying a screaming child out of the house at 7:15 in the morning (sorry, neighbors) because he wanted to put his shoes on himself and I had to do it.

It's like talking to a completely incompetent human being. Oh, wait. Silly me. It's not "like." It is. BECAUSE 3-YEAR-OLDS ARE COMPLETELY INCOMPETENT HUMAN BEINGS.

You see, 3-year-olds aren't all that great at remembering that there are other people in the world. They don't really want to know how else anything is done besides the way they want to do it:

Me: You have to pull the tongue of the shoe out, you see? Your shoe magically fits now.

3-year-old [starting over]: No! That's not how you do it!

They can't really compute that not everything in the world is going to go their way:

3-year-old: I want the purple plate. [Gets the blue plate, because a purple plate doesn't even exist. Cries for the next half hour because of a plate that doesn't exist].

They don't know how to learn from their mistakes:

Me: Sit down. I don't want you to fall.

[3-year-old stays standing and falls out of his chair, out of his brother's chair and face first onto the hard tile floor. Console him and make sure he isn't really hurt.]

Me: See. That wouldn't have happened if you had been sitting down. Now get back in your seat and sit down on your bottom.

[Turn around to cut the last strawberries. Turn back around to see 3-year-old still standing in almost the exact position he was before, except this time he's dancing on one foot.]

I've discovered that finding humor in the speech mistakes my 3-year-olds make is one of the only things that keeps me from walking out on them when they're fighting for forty-five minutes about whether the exact same Lightning McQueen cars are the dark red Lightning McQueen or the light red Lightning McQueen. (The answer is neither. They're the EXACT SAME CAR, for God's sake.)

So I've made this handy little list so I can remember and laugh and find my way back into thanks for these two 3-year-olds who fill my house with ~~mayhem~~ laughter.

1. Demands.

These can sound calm, like a simple, "Get me some milk" or "I need my shoes" or "I want a peach." Or they can come from a belligerent 3-year-old who's been taught the correct way to ask but just won't, because 3-year-olds.

3-year-old: Get me some milk.

Me: …

3-year-old: I firsty.

Me: Nice to meet you, firsty.

3-year-old: Get me some milk, Mama. [A little louder this time]

Me: I don't do anything for boys who demand.

3-year-old: I NEED MILK!

Me: Not when you ask like that.

3-year-old: GET ME MILK, MAMA!

I can play this game all day, because it usually happens at dinner and I've got my wine.

2. Buts.

Every parent's nightmare. Or at least this parent's. I have some strong-willed 3-year-olds, and I hear a whole lot of buts.

Me: It's time to brush your teeth.

3-year-old: But I not finished playing.

Me: I know it's hard to quit playing. Right now it's time to brush your teeth.

3-year-old: But we dinnent eat durnner.

Me: Yes we did. You had five pieces of pizza.

3-year-old: But we dinnent get to play.

Me: What are you doing right now?

3-year-old:

Me:

3-year-old: But I need a drink.

Me: Go brush your teeth.

Other 3-year-old [eats half the toothpaste while I'm occupied with his twin brother.]

There are also the buts that don't make sense.

Me: It's time to go upstairs, where you're supposed to be.

3-year-old: But my cup is itchy.

Something tells me I don't want to know what that means.

Me: Please don't leave the door open.

3-year-old: But my eyes are tired.

Me: Don't chew on your shoes. It's really gross.

3-year-old: But my legs are itchy.

I wonder why. *Shudder*

3. Completely wrong words.

My twins have great vocabularies, because we read a lot, and, also, they have older brothers who talk nonstop. The problem is, they haven't really paid attention to the context in which those words are used. So their tries sound something like this:

3-year-old: I dinnent do my hisand today.

Me: You didn't what?

3-year-old: I dinnent do my hisand today.

Me: I have no idea what you're saying. Do we have an interpreter available?

3-year-old: I DINNENT DO MY HISAND TODAY.

8-year-old: He's saying he didn't do his highs and lows today.

Good thing there are older brothers.

3-year-old: I sweatering really bad.

Me: You're what?

3-year-old: I sweatering really bad.

Me: You mean you're sweating?

3-year-old: Yeah. I sweatering.

So close.

3-year-old: I have to very poo poo.

Me: …

4. Consonants

Consonants are not the friends of 3-year-olds in certain instances. Those certain instances would be words like "costume," which will become "cossayume;" "actually," which will become "ashaly;" and "shirt," which will become "sh*t" (You'll want to have a video camera trained on the kid who does this. You may even want to make a Christmas video with the kid saying, "Oh, shirt! Merry Christmas!" and send it to all your friends and family, which we definitely did not do. I'm just throwing out ideas here.)

For all their arguing and mispronouncing and demanding, 3-year-olds can be ~~twerps~~ truly delightful little people. I'm really glad I have two of them, and I'm not looking forward to their fourth birthday at all, because, dang, I just want them to stay 3 forever and ever and ever.

I'll just say what every other parent of a 3-year-old is thinking: Sometimes it's a good thing time marches on.

It's the End of the (School) Year As We Know It

I was done with school long before the year ended.

The early-morning schedule gets old by week #2, because boys like to sleep until at least 8 (unless it's the weekend, and then they're up at 5:30), and school starts at 7:45 a.m., and that tardy bell rings strong and fierce, and even though it's only three who must be there on time, all the others have to get up, too, because the three make enough tornado noise trying to find a backpack he's sitting on (if you're the 5-year-old), complaining about what's for breakfast (if you're the 7-year-old), and bemoaning the fact that he has no more sweat pants that are clean (if you're the 9-year-old) that everybody wakes right along with them.

The homework gets old by week #4, because what 7-year-old remembers that he has some math worksheets he has to do when there are LEGOs in the house, and who can even concentrate on reading a passage and answering some silly questions about it when your brothers keep running through the kitchen screeching like spider monkeys dressed in Robin Hood costumes or when they keep exclaiming over the cool fort they constructed from a box or they are, heaven forbid, reading aloud from a book?

Homework at 7 is like adding another line onto a parent's to-do list: Keep boy on task even though he's used up his on-task capabilities in the seven hours he was at school today.

Believe me, my to-do list was massive enough already without this extra line. I mean, someone has to sit on the couch and read a book every now and then, and it might as well be me.

We were done with all the on-grade reader books by about week #12. All my boys are fantastic readers who read whatever they want all the time here at home. They read Pokemon graphic novels and Bill Watterson comics and the newest Elephant & Piggie books. Which is why we stopped signing those log-their-reading folders right around the beginning of December. It looks like none of them have picked up a book since Dec. 3. They have. I promise. I just can't always find a pen. Or remember which one read what. Or find the actual folders, because boys are so good at putting things where they belong. The chances of all three of those happening at the same time are very, very rare.

AND THEN THE PAPERS.

So many papers.

There are advertisements for sports camps and karate programs and dance lessons all throughout the year. There are all the worksheets a first-grader and kindergartener and third grader do. There are amazing works of art they paint and draw and color that come home from their art class. There are essays and teacher notes and lunch charge reminders that we owe the school some money.

We did fairly well with all those papers for about the first twenty-four weeks of school. I was actually pretty proud we lasted that long. We had a system: sort them, store them, or toss them in the recycling. "Store them" ended up breaking down a bit, because I'd start putting the whole stack of papers in the "store them" pile so I could "look at them later," except later never really came back around.

And when February swept in, we just stopped caring.

I don't even know if it was a gradual not-caring or an all-at-once not-caring, but now those papers sit on the bottom shelf of our coffee table or on the library shelves covering up the spines of books or between the beds in the twins' room (they thought paper might work for insulation and smuggled some in their room without our noticing. The papers are now tiny, tiny little pieces that will have to be hand-picked from the carpet because our vacuum cleaner sucks but doesn't really. Thanks for the gift guys. I now feel like setting the house on fire.).

The paper hills have become paper mountains. Soon, we'll be able to repair all the things that are wrong with our house with paper. Hole in the wall? Cover it with paper. Fan is missing a blade? Construct one out of paper. No more toilet paper? WE HAVE PLENTY OF PAPER!

The end of the school year is a bittersweet time, because it holds the sadness of a school year ending and a child getting older, or at least seeming to get older, and the (mostly unspoken) fear of having said child home ALL HOURS OF ALL THE DAYS ALL SUMMER.

But when I weigh the sad and the afraid and the glad, I think I am mostly glad, because the be-an-involved-school-parent pressure and the papers will stay far, far away. Mostly I'm glad because my sons are brilliant and funny and delightful, and I'm going to enjoy their around-all-day presence for all of 2.3 hours on the first day.

Today is the last day of school, the last day we get up early, the day books will no longer come home and homework will stay in a classroom until next year. Which means tomorrow boys will sleep late and they will play together well, because they missed each other so much, and they will spend quiet time in their alone places so I don't even have to remind them to get "back where you're supposed to be."

Well, you know, a mom can always hope.

Hey Kids: Just Because It's Summer Doesn't Mean You Can Do Whatever You Want

It's the fourteenth time he's come to our room tonight, and we still have to get up at 5 in the morning to get anything done, so his daddy leads him out and says, "It's time for you to go to bed, for the last time."

"But I don't have school," he says, as if we didn't just have this conversation fifteen minutes ago. "It's my summer break."

Oh, well, in that case, why don't you stay up all night, and, while you're at it, go ahead and disregard all the rules, because IT'S SUMMER VACATION!

When I tilt my head and squint my eyes just so, I can almost understand why my kids would equate summer vacation with do-whatever-I-want time, because summer means they are no longer trapped at school for seven whole hours, listening to someone else giving instructions. They don't have to write their name on fifty math or reading or science worksheets, and they don't have a half-hour time limit on lunch, and they don't have to finish all their work before they get to do the fun stuff like reading and drawing and playing.

But what's getting old in my house is that every day there's another fight—not because we're coming up against new territory. No. We're coming up against the same old territory that the boys have forgotten because apparently summertime is synonymous with short-term memory loss.

Dang summertime.

Sometimes I wish summertime meant exactly what they think it means—relaxation of the rules. I really do.

But last time I relaxed the rules and let them have a little more freedom, they pulled out the economy-sized glitter I didn't even know we had for some horrifying glitter projects we're still cleaning up, a year later. Also, the 8-year-old somehow climbed to the top of the bathroom door, where he positioned a cup of water so it would fall on someone's head when they opened the door. And someone else put thumbtacks in the twins' booster seats.

So no. Rules still intact.

I wrote a note for my boys, reminding them of the most-frequently-forgotten rules. Feel free to use this letter as many times as you need. I've already read it to them twenty-six times today, because that's how often they've forgotten.

Dear kids,

It's summertime. Not I'm-a-grownup-now time.

Unfortunately, that means there are still rules in our house. Here are some you seem to have forgotten:

1. No, you may not snack all day.

We just had breakfast, and you ate twelve pancakes and five eggs. How in the world are you still hungry fifteen minutes later? That's called boredom, son. Boredom is not a good excuse to eat. Get thee outside. Thou shalt dig in some dirt. Or do art (without glitter). Or read one of your books. Or chew on your fingers. Whatever keeps you out of the refrigerator. Because, good Lord. The grocery store only has so much food.

2. Close the door behind you.

This rule has been in place since you were old enough to walk, but you've conveniently picked now, when it's so hot it's painful to wear clothes, to forget? That's called irony, kids. It's ironic that you've forgotten how to close a door in the middle of summer.

Here. I'll help you out. Closing is quite easy once you understand the mechanics of it. So allow me to explain: If you push the door to open it, you'll push the door *away* from you to close it. Push it away from you. Away from you. Away from you. There. Hear that sound? That's the sound of a door closing. Amazing, isn't it?

Now that we've had this nice little refresher, next time you leave the door open, I'll take a portion of the electricity bill out of your college fund. You won't be laughing when you're 18 and you don't have enough money to pay for your first semester of books (because, by the time college rolls around, that's about what the money we've saved will be worth. If you keep forgetting to close the door, it'll pay for your first dinner out.).

3. No, you may not stay up all night.

Believe it or not, even though you're not going to school for the time being, we are still concerned that you get enough sleep—because we love you, and we know sleep is important for you to grow and function well. Also (mostly) because you turn into a horrid monster when you haven't had enough sleep. So turn out the light. Put away the book.

And for God's sake, stop coming to our room when we're almost asleep, asking if we remember where you left your special pencil with the blue eraser. Some people want to get some sleep around here.

4. Things that were not allowed before are also not allowed now.

This would be things like walking across the table with dirty, dirty feet; getting five games out that, all together, have a total of forty-thousand pieces; sneaking onto the computer to play your Cool Math game when a parent is not present and before you've earned your technology time.

Nope. Still not allowed in summer.

What? Every other kid gets to do what you can't? Well, it's too bad those aren't your parents. You got stuck with us. It's a hard knock life.

5. Any mess you make, you still clean it up.

What's that? You dumped out all the glitter on accident? Well, it's a good thing you know how to wipe off a table and sweep a floor, so get to it.

Wait, you want to play outside with your friend, but you were playing throw-them-in-the-air-and-see-where-they-fall with the markers? Welp. You know the rules. Clean it up first.

You don't like this game and want to play a different one? CLEAN IT UP.

6. You may not wear your swimsuit for more than twenty days in a row.

It's time for a dress code, kids. I know your swimsuits are comfortable and you're hoping that, by wearing them every hour of every day, we'll say, oh, look, it's time to go to the pool, but no. A swimsuit is not an appropriate choice for twenty consecutive days. I'll give you five. Maybe even six.

It's been longer than that, so let me have them. Let me have them. LET ME HAVE THEM. I just need to wash them, and then you can have them for another six days. Now. Go get your underwear on. Remember the other unspoken rule: No skivvies, no service.

7. Pool time is not bath time.

I know, I know. Chlorine, soap, what's the difference? It's so fun to play in the pool and pretend it's a bath, and it's no fun to come home and get wet again in a tiny little bath tub. But the thing is, chlorine. And kids peeing. And all those other bodies.

A dip in the pool does not qualify for a bath. Get on out. Come home. And wash those smelly armpits (you too, kids.).

8. If you know the rules and break them, there will (still) be consequences.

I know it's hard to believe that your parents are still enforcing these stupid rules even though it's summertime and you should really only be experiencing great freedom and wonderful fun, but you see kids? Consistency is important, too. Without consistency, you would feel like you were trying to navigate life without an anchor tethering you to reality. Living life without an anchor isn't as much fun as you think. Just ask any kid without a parent.

I know these rules seem ridiculous and arbitrary, but we enforce them because we want you to have the best possible family life experience you can. We have them because, more than anything, we love you.

Now. Go play outside so I can have a little quiet time and try to remember why these rules are so important.

Five Different Eating Personalities of Children

My husband and I used to sit down to a quiet dinner, just the two of us. We used to be able to eat the same thing every week. We used to be able to hold hands when we wanted and pack up leftovers for the next day's lunch.

Kids changed all that.

Now we sit down to a dinner with more words than you'll read in a George R.R. Martin novel. We have to have something different every night of the month. We use our hands to dish out food, and there are never any leftovers.

Over the years of eating dinners together—which, in spite of the mayhem six boys can rouse, we still find important—my boys have shown themselves to have several different eating personalities. Because I'm a proud parent, I've recorded them for you below.

There is **The Picky Eater.**

This is the kid who asks what's for dinner, and, before you even get "chicken noodle soup" out, he's already looked in the pot and is saying, "I want something else."

"If you can cook it," I'll say. (He can't. He's 4.)

"But I HATE that."

"Do you even know what it is?" I'll say. (Also, I'm a cook, not a chef, kid.)

"No."

I have to give him credit. He gives it a chance. In fact, he gives it three chances, in three separate helpings, all the while saying how much he wishes he could have something else for dinner.

We also have **The Player**.

This is the kid who will take a string of spaghetti and swing it around like a rope. He'll set up a forest with his broccoli. He will wear his pizza like a triangle hat.

"Stop playing with your food," I'll say.

"I not playing," he'll say. "I eating. See?" He'll put the broccoli in his mouth, shouting, "I eat tree! Oh no!"

Well, at least he's eating broccoli.

And we have his twin brother, **The Wanderer**.

This is the kid who cannot put one bite in his mouth without moving from the table to pick up the book he wanted to show his brothers. He'll take another bite and remember he forgot to show Mama the toy he found under the couch today. It was gone for so long. Another bite, and he's up again, using the bathroom or putting his shoes where they go or remembering he left his Thermos in the refrigerator.

"The rule is you stay at the table and ask to be excused," I'll say.

"I *am* staying at the table," he'll say.

"You're not."

"I AM!"

"No. That's not staying. See? You just got up from the table."

"No! I staying."

Ever argue with a 2-year-old? Not only does it not make sense, YOU WILL NOT WIN.

So we strapped him into a booster seat. The Wanderer wanders no more.

One of our boys is **The Talker**.

This is the kid who will take so excruciatingly long to eat his dinner he's the last one at the table and we've all fallen asleep.

It's not that he isn't hungry, because he'll always ask for more, even if dinner has already been cleaned up. For three hours. It's just that he has to tell us every single detail of every single second of his day, and he forgets that there is food to eat. The loud rumbling in his belly will not make him shovel that food any faster.

"You should eat," I'll say, after he's told me in finite detail what went on today in his Sage class today and how someone thought it would be a good idea to sharpen his finger and he spent the rest of the afternoon in the nurse's office trying to control the bleeding (Not really. That didn't actually happen at all. I just can't remember what exactly he told me because my mind started wandering after Word Four Hundred Seventy-Three. But once he told a really long story about how he and one of his friends dared each other to stand in an ant hill for five minutes, after which I asked him "What were you thinking," to which he replied [shrug]).

"But I want to tell you about my day."

Twenty-five minutes of words about every person he came across at school today and what he did in math class and who he played with at recess and I'm getting a nervous tick in my leg, because dinner is almost over and he's only taken two bites.

Don't get me wrong. I'm glad he talks. It's just...Eat.

Then there is **The Inhaler**.

This kid is the opposite of The Talker. He will start eating at the exact same time everyone else does but will finish when everyone else is on their third bite.

"May I have some more please?" he'll say.

"You're already done?" I'll say.

"I'm really hungry," he'll say.

Clearly.

These are the only words The Inhaler will say during dinner, except for a quick one-word answer when asked what his thankful is for the day. He's too busy shoveling food to talk.

"Chew your food," I'll say. "Take your time."

He'll shoot me that you-don't-know-what-you're-talking-about look.

"My stomach hurts," he'll say after dinner.

"Do you think it's because you ate too much?" I'll say. "Too fast?"

"No. I think it's just gas."

I'll wait a while before I tell him that eating too fast causes gas.

All I know is mealtime sure has gotten interesting. And, if I'm being honest, a whole lot better.

What Summer Looks Like in a House Full of Kids

This school year went by way too fast.

And now all my boys are at home, all together for every hour of every day for the next several months. It's the first time we've encountered this boy-count for a significant stretch of time since we had our sixth boy in January.

I tell you, I don't know if I'm going to make it.

Naturally, I woke up that first morning with a massive headache, because life is hilariously unfair like that. There was a foreboding that was more than just the headache, too, right behind my eyes, because I've been entrenched in edits for a middle grade novel and the house is a disaster and the boys came home with all their leftover supplies and fifty-thousand pieces of paper yesterday.

So I had my suspicions about how this day would go.

Here's a rundown of the highlights:

5 a.m.—I get out of bed to write for a couple of hours before the boys are expected up between 7:30 and 8 a.m., because they're surely going to sleep late this first day of summer vacation. Oh, idealism. How I hate you.

5:12 a.m.—The baby starts fussing, even though he usually sleeps until 8.

5:19 a.m.—The baby goes back to sleep.

5:42 a.m.—I hear thumping footsteps. Surely not.

6 a.m.—Still writing, but those footsteps are sounding more and

more suspicious.

6:17 a.m.—Now I have to investigate, because it's completely quiet. That never means anything good.

6:24 a.m.—(Because it takes that long to get down the stairs with a stupid boot cast. I broke my foot a couple of weeks ago.). I find them, one school boy and his next-in-line brother using the scissors they left out last night to cut tiny little confetti-sized pieces of paper out of the 5-year-old's final kindergarten report card.

6:31 a.m.—I start breakfast, trying not to stare at all.those.pieces of paper. The awake boys disappear, and before I'm three minutes into fixing breakfast, they've woken every other boy in the house, and the walls are already shaking.

6: 34 a.m.—I'm hungry, Mama. Yes, I know, I'm working as fast as I can. May I have an apple while I'm waiting? No, you may not—this will be done soon. But Mama, I'm starving!

6:35 a.m.—I try to listen to the talking ones and get breakfast started while trying to keep the twins out of the markers and glue sticks and sharpened pencils that have multiplied seemingly overnight.

6:43 a.m.—Someone throws a pillow at someone else and accidentally breaks a picture. Clean it up.

6:48 a.m.—Someone dumps out the entire bin of LEGO pieces on the dining room table where the clothes were all folded and ready to be put away. Seriously, guys. BREAKFAST IS ALMOST DONE. JUST SIT IN YOUR CHAIRS.

6:56 a.m.—Smoothies are ready! Come get them at the table. Eggs will be done shortly.

6:57 a.m.—A twin plays with his fork and knocks his smoothie cup off the table. Clean it up.

7:04 a.m.—The eggs are ready! Watch out, it's hot. Blow on it before you eat it. (Fantasize about how maybe this will give me 4.7 minutes of relaxation time.)

7:07 a.m.—We're done! Let's dump out more LEGOs!

7:09 a.m.—Mama, may I have some milk? Will you play LEGOs with me? Will you come outside with me? I want to color, Mama. Too many people talking at the same time. Lock myself in the bathroom.

7:12 a.m.—Yeah, that was a bad idea. One of the twins found the one hundred fifty manuscript pages I brought downstairs (wishful thinking that I'd actually get a chance to work on them) and made it rain paper. I realize too late that I forgot to number the pages and now I'll have a puzzle to put together. Just what I wanted.

7:34 a.m.—Turn on an audio book. It usually quiets them for a while.

8 a.m.—Feed the baby while they are (mercifully!) still listening to the audio book.

8:02 a.m.—The 6-year-old skips to the refrigerator to get an apple, even though he just had two smoothies and three eggs an hour ago. Um, no.

8:17 a.m.—Baby is finished, twins ask fifteen times for more crayons.

8:20 a.m.—Twins decide paper isn't working for them today and now choose to color in one of their brother's library books he left on the table.

8:31 a.m.—Someone leaves the door open. I yell at him to close it. It will not be the last time I get to practice my delivery, though. I will get to perfect it six thousand other times this morning. I discovered there are quite a few variations of this popular phrase:

"Shut the door, please."

"Please shut the door."

"Close the door, guys."

"Hey, guys, close the door."

"Ohmygosh, close the door."

"Hey! How about you close the door?"

"How many times do I have to tell you to CLOSE THE DOOR?"

"Are you forgetting something? How about CLOSING THE DOOR?"

"CLOSE THE DOOR, DANG IT!"

I love my boys just as much as any other mother, and I really am excited about having the bigger ones home for the summer, because they're awesome people and I enjoy talking with them anytime I feel like it. But the dynamic of six home at the same time, asking for something, getting into things, leaving the door open is just…crazy.

It wasn't all crazy, though. It was also really fun and beautiful and wonderful.

I got to see them play with LEGOs together, constructing fire worlds and ice worlds and grass worlds together. I got to see them waiting at the table when I came down to make breakfast, dressed as Spider-Man and Starscream. I got to see the 5-year-old read a story to his little brothers and run to kiss "his baby" whenever he felt like it. I got to see the 8-year-old settle into an old story, and I got to laugh with him about how the boy in the story told his school counselor that he likes to eat dog food, and I got to see him teach his twin brothers how to build a LEGO car that actually works.

It really wasn't nearly as bad as I thought it would be.
Of course there's always tomorrow.

The Days That Only Come Round Once a Year (We Hope)

What Happens When Kids Are Detoxing From the Grandparents

It's their first day back from the grandparents' house after a week of running wild outside in the country and swimming in a pool and watching movies for Quiet Time, and my boys have forgotten how to act.

We are incredibly blessed that my mom and stepdad took the older three boys for a week (and do every summer) and that my father-in-law took the Dennis-the-Menace-times-two twins for a few days (because that's about all the time anyone can handle with these guys), but man. Detoxing stinks.

My parents eat a lot like us—no processed food, lots of fruits and veggies, no special "treat" with every meal. So I can't even blame it on the food (which is my usual culprit). But when they come back from Nonny and Poppy's house, my boys are bouncing off the walls (and that's an understatement.). No one wants to go into the backyard when I suggest bouncing on the trampoline instead, because they all missed their toys "so, so, so much!"

No one remembers where to put their shoes (the shoe basket we've had by the door for YEARS). They don't even remember how to get dressed. It's as if dressing for seven days in a row is enough effort to last the entire summer.

The first day of detox was the third son's fifth birthday, which means tradition set a birthday treat in front of him at breakfast. I had a feeling it was a bad idea, but what are you going to do with tradition? Ten minutes later they were catapulting over the side of the couch so quickly I didn't know whose name to call out in my scolding, because they were all blurs, and by the time I remembered one name, another was already in the middle of his performance.

They got crayons, coloring books, Hot Wheels and a bin of four million LEGOs out all at the same time, even though we have a very important rule about "only one thing out at a time."

"I'd like to see one of you build something with LEGOs, color a picture, and play with the cars all at the same time," I said.

They looked at me like I'd lost my mind. (By that point, I already had.)

After dinner, they forgot how to put their plates and silverware away.

"We used paper plates at Nonny and Poppy's house," they said when I asked.

"But Nonny didn't make you throw them away?" I said.

"Yeah," they said, not noticing the glaring inconsistency here: They still had to carry their plates somewhere.

There is just something about not being in the house where your parents live that makes you forget all the rules. Or, worse, make up your own.

Detoxing day one was filled with rules amended by incompetent-at-logic children. Here are just a few of them.

Actual rule: Only one book down from the shelves at a time.

Amended rule by detoxing, too-creative-for-his-own-good 8-year-old: Except when I create this world called Animalia. You see, Mama? I brought all my twelve thousand stuffed animals up from the garage where I found them in a trash bag—why were they in a trash bag?—and made my room like a stuffed animal resort. They have a reading corner here. See? There's a book for every one of them. I'll clean it all up, don't worry.

Yeah, right.

Actual rule: Before you get something else out to play with, clean up whatever it was you were playing with before.

Amended rule by detoxing, I'm-the-birthday-boy 5-year-old: Except I get to pick everything to play with for the day AND I don't have to clean anything up, because I'm the birthday boy. What's that, Mama? It's clean up time? Well, I'm the birthday boy, so I don't have to clean up. Nuh-uh. I don't have to clean up even though I got to pick all the toys. I'm the birthday boy and I LOVE NOT CLEANING UP! IT SHOULD BE MY BIRTHDAY EVERY DAY FOREVER!

(Don't ever promise a birthday boy he's exempt from cleaning up.)

Actual rule: Stay at the table until you're finished with your food and we say yes to your "May I be excused?" question.

Amended rule by detoxing, I-can't-stop-moving-my-feet 6-year-old: Except that I forgot to show you this really neat picture I made at Nonny and Poppy's house, and did you see this word search I colored instead of circling words on, and, oh, yeah, I made this really neat paper airplane out of a superhero drawing. Do you want to see it fly? And my brother just got new markers for his birthday and I have this blank sheet of white paper and I LOVE TO COLOR SO MUCH!

Please. Stop.

Actual rule: Don't touch the CD player when you're only 3.

Amended rule by detoxing, strong-willed 3-year-old twin: Except I'm an annoying 3-year-old who won't listen to anything you have to say. Touch, touch, touch. See me touch?

"Stop touching it," I say.

Touch, touch, touch.

[Sit him on the couch while I sit beside him acknowledging that I understand he really, really, really wants to touch those buttons and that I really wish I could let him but he could break the CD player touching them all. Let him up three minutes later.]

Touch, touch, touch.

Long, long sigh.

Actual rule: Body excrement belongs in the toilet. Please, for the love of God, don't poop in your underwear.

Amended rule by detoxing I'm-the-other-menace 3-year-old: Oops.

I finally had to lock them all in the backyard just to regain my sanity.

I am incredibly grateful for the time our boys get to spend with their grandparents, no matter how challenging it is to get them back on a schedule and remind them of the rules they've known since the beginning of time (at least their time). They are not only spending valuable time with another generation but they are also giving their daddy and me the opportunity to spend some beautiful time by ourselves, reconnecting and engaging in conversations where we actually get to finish our sentences and remembering how much we liked each other in the first place.

The time we spend detoxing is definitely worth that reconnection. Every single time.

P.S. Just power through that first day, Mama and Daddy. It will get better. Remember? It always does (not before you add a few gray hairs, though). Pretty soon you'll be right back to counting down the days until you can send them away again.

Why Traveling with Kids is Maybe the Worst Idea Ever

We're finally all packed up, and everyone is buckled and already said their piece about how strange it is that Mama's driving this time (because I never choose to), and Daddy has his laptop open, ready to work. We're going to get moving, after two hours of trying.

That's right. It takes two hours just to leave the house.

And then.

Then I turn on the car. The gas light, indicating a gas tank on fumes, is on.

Son of a—

I know what this means. A stop. A stop that will likely turn into a potty break that will turn into five potty breaks (because everyone forgot to go before we left) that will turn into thirty minutes (or more!) of wasted time.

It's only a three-hour trip. It will take us five (not counting the two-hour departure time).

When we stop, after I've huffed and puffed about how someone should fill up the car once in a while and why can't whoever was driving it last just fill it up before the gas light comes on (pretty sure it was me, that day I was running late to get dinner started and the three older boys had just effectively made me lose my mind fighting over two computers in the public library, so I didn't want to stay in the car with them one second longer), I tell them we are NOT getting out to potty, because this is not a scheduled potty break. This is an inconvenient, necessary stop.

Scheduled potty breaks happen when the baby needs to eat.

"But I really need to go!" the 8-year-old says. It's been a whopping three minutes since we left.

"Did you go before you left, like I told you?" I say.

"I didn't have to go then," he says.

Welp, you don't have to go now, either.

There are so many kids. It's like a field trip traveling with all these boys. When one needs to potty, they all do. When one falls asleep, the others don't. They just get louder.

Every two minutes a different one asks, "Are we almost there?"

We're not even out of the neighborhood yet.

At first we answered no. Then we answered yes. Then we tried to ignore it. Then we told them to stop asking. Then we told them the truth.

"Two more hours."

"One hour and fifty-eight minutes."

"One hour and fifty-six minutes."

Then we turned it into math practice.

"One hour and fifty-four minutes. How many minutes have passed since you last asked?"

"One hour and fifty-two minutes. Do you notice a pattern between your questions?"

(This plan backfired, because they actually adore math.)

In the end, this is the question that will break us. It's the one that will make Husband and me look at each other with those crazy eyes and silently mouth, "Never, ever, ever, ever, ever, ever, ever, EVER again," so the kids can't hear our declaration and have a meltdown in the middle of our meltdown (the car would explode if too many meltdowns happen at the same time. It's a law of physics.).

I took some traveling notes on things I wanted to make sure I'd remember next time I think it would be a good idea to pack six boys into the van and travel more than the five miles to the grocery store:

1. Bring some oversized cups.

It's never too early for boys to learn the art of peeing in cups. When our 3-year-old twins are playing free at home, they will go hours without having to visit the restroom. When they're in the car, their bladders shrink to about the size of a peanut. They need to pee every half hour. So make it a game: They have to pee in a cup without unbuckling.

On second thought, you'll probably be the loser in the end, so let's just forget I mentioned it.

2. Bring treats for every mile you go without hearing, "Are we almost there?"

This question (and its twin: "How much longer until we get there?") will drive you absolutely crazy, because when you have multiple children, they each take turns asking, as if the answer you gave their brother wasn't good enough for them. As if their asking might suddenly create a time warp we can speed through that crosses fifty miles in one minute (Every parent wishes this time warp were Real Life instead of Science Fiction.). As if something has changed in one hundred twenty seconds.

One kid might ask it two thousand times. Six kids ask it 13 billion times. So reward them for keeping their mouths shut.

3. Don't bother putting shoes on the 3-year-olds.

They take them off as soon as they get in the car anyway, and they'll get buried under all the jackets that somehow keep ending up in the car even though it's two hundred degrees outside. Some of them will get shuffled under seats. One will probably fall out the door and you won't notice (true story). You'll waste way too much time (and remember: minutes are precious when traveling with kids) looking for shoes, especially when one has gone missing because it was left in the last town. So don't bother.

4. Bring audio books. They're more for you than for the kids.

They're so the next time they ask, "Are we almost there?" you can say, "I'm trying to listen to the story." They're so when they say they need to go to the potty again you can say, "Let's wait until this story is over (they don't have to know that will be another hour). They're so when they're rocking the back of the car because they want to move it faster, you can retreat into your own world and try to ignore the way the van is not moving any faster—probably slower, because everything is slower with children when children try to help.

5. DON'T INTRODUCE I SPY. OR KNOCK KNOCK JOKES.

Notice this one is in caps. There's a good reason for that. Three thousand rounds of I Spy. Five hundred knock knock jokes. Do you remember? Of course you do. Your eye is still twitching.

The "Are we almost there" question is nothing compared to this. So just close your mouth and keep your eyes on the road.

6. Use a better reservation system than Husband.

"Shoot," Husband says when we're turning into our destination. The sky fell dark hours ago, the kids are tired, and I'm feeling especially grumpy, because I had to drive.

"What?" I say.

"Never mind," he says. But I know. There's something. We've been married too long for him to hide anything from me.

"What?" I say again. I've got a bad feeling about this.

"Well, I can't remember which condo is ours."

At this point nothing could really surprise me. I don't even blow up or rant about how could you not write it down and do I have to do everything and how about we just turn around and go back home. I'm too tired for all that. So I simply put my head down on the steering wheel and let loose a long, long sigh.

"They left the key under the mat," he says, looking at the row of fifty condos.

"Have fun looking," I say.

He gets out, checks enough doormats to make it halfway down the line of condos, then returns to the car.

At the last minute he remembered. It was the first condo we passed through the gate.

We all pile into the 500-square-foot condo that looked bigger in the online pictures and collapse on our bed.

Nothing like traveling together to ensure a good nights' sleep.

School Shopping with Kids is Just as Hellish as it Sounds

Every year in Texas there's this wonderful weekend where shoppers get to take advantage of tax-free shopping on school supplies and clothes. Hundreds of thousands of people head out in droves, hitting all the local stores and cleaning out school supplies and every rack of clothes those stores possibly have stocked—all within the first three hours of tax-free weekend.

I just love large crowds with all those excited kids who aren't mine, weaving in and out of the guarantees-an-anxiety-attack-aisles, so, of course, I'm always one of them. Because, you know, tax-free weekend saves me five dollars and forty-seven cents. Totally worth it.

This year my mom offered to take my 3-year-old twins for the weekend so I could take the three going-to-school ones out for a few necessities and a handful of new clothes (because their jeans are now capris).

Strangely enough, I always look forward to this day. It's sort of a tradition in our house now, the squeezing through sweaty crowds to get that perfect Spider-Man backpack, the yelling at my kids because they picked out five lunch boxes and they only need one, the robot-like explanation (because it's so oft repeated) that their daddy and I have a thing called a budget, and this little personalized pencil with a neon green zipper bag is not in that budget. And every time tax-free weekend starts creeping up on us, I can't sleep for days I'm so excited, almost as if I'm shopping for me (I'm not. I haven't shopped for me in eight years).

Let me just tell you what you probably already know: Shopping with kids is like walking through hell with a checkbook.

And yet, every year I forget the horror that was last year, and I convince myself that this year will surely be different, because the boys are older and more mature, and they understand the whole budget thing better and, because of all this, they won't annoy me twelve seconds after we get to the store.

We started out well, a whole nine hundred seconds of not-annoying. We stopped first at an arts and crafts store, where we picked out a chalkboard and some chalk markers their daddy could use to hand-letter their morning routines, personalized and artsy (incentive for getting out of bed on school mornings: they get to see art!). They helped me put the chalkboard and chalk pens carefully in the cart, and we headed for the register and paid with little or no fuss beyond their asking if they could please, please, please look at the Beanie Boos, just real quick. Okay, I said, because they were so good.

And then there was Target.

Now. I love Target. It's the closest department store to my house, so it's where I get the majority of things like paper towels and toilet paper and replacement toothbrushes after I caught one of the 3-year-old twins trying to scrub-clean the toilet with the existing ones and then putting them all in his mouth ("Look at my teef!" he said, and I threw up a little.).

The first thing they asked when we walked through the sliding doors was whether we could go look at the toys.

Um, no. We're here for school stuff, I said. We're on a time budget. And a money budget.

My mom had already bought the kids' school supplies this year, so all we really needed were a few clothes, some shoes, a backpack, and lunch supplies for all of them. We went to the lunch box section first and spied the Thermoses. Two of them already had Thermoses, so we only needed one.

"But I want this one," said one of the already-have-a-perfectly-fine Thermos boys.

"No," I said. "You already have one."

"But look at this one," he said. "It's really cool."

"Well, too bad it wasn't here last year," I said and put it back on the shelf.

Half an hour later, when I finally pulled them away from the Thermos shelf, we wheeled over to the backpacks, where three other mothers were wrestling backpacks from their children's hands.

"Only one," they were saying.

Oh, man. Here we go.

I leaned against my cart, trying to empathize with all those poor mothers, while my boys pulled every boy-looking backpack off the racks—Transformers, Darth Vader, Batman, Superman, some dog I've never seen before, Super Mario Brothers, Spider-Man, Ninja Turtles, everything you could possibly imagine—one after the other falling at my feet.

"Look at this one, Mama!" they would periodically say. "I want this one!"

They knew they were only getting one backpack, so I didn't feel the need to repeat what we'd already explicitly talked through on the way here. So I just let them bring their choices to me, after which I'd say, "Is this the one you want?" and when they said no, I'd hang it back up. I would have made my boys put the rejected candidates back in their rightful place, but the first one who tried knocked the entire rack of backpacks onto the floor. I thought I'd save myself a little trouble.

Fast forward another hour, and they had their backpacks stuffed with their lunch boxes and strapped to their backs, because they wanted to carry them instead of putting them in the cart. That lasted about three minutes, and then they tossed them into the cart. Mostly because, sandwiched right between the school supplies section and the clothes at our Target is the toys section.

Come on, Target. Give a mom a break.

I lost two of the three boys, but by this time, I was already so annoyed and ready to be done I just left them. They knew where we were going. So only one hung to the side of the basket—until he realized that his brothers were gone. This one got lost one time and gets really scared when any of his brothers disappear, so of course we had to go back to pry his brothers loose from the LEGO aisle.

"Let's go, guys," I said. "Not what we're here for."

"Can we get one LEGO set, Mama? To celebrate the start of school?" the 8-year-old said.

He's clever, but we've never "just bought" a LEGO set for any occasion, I said. So no.

They hopped back on the side of the cart, which collectively weighed one hundred thirty pounds. Have you ever tried to push a one-hundred-thirty-pound cart with a screwy wheel? (I always pick the screwy-wheeled ones, even if the carts are brand new. Want to snag a perfectly working cart at the store? Just stand in line behind me and wait until I pick one.) People kept passing us giving us dirty looks, because we were, after all, on a shopper's highway, and I was going well below the speed limit, using every muscle in my arms just to turn the corner.

Finally we reached the clothes. This is where it really fell apart.

I don't even know what happened. I only remember one boy who wears extra small holding up an extra-large shirt and saying he wanted to buy it, and then the boy who wears medium holding up an extra small and saying he wanted this one and then the one who wears small holding up a large, saying this was the one he most definitely wanted to take home, and I had the luxury of telling them all that they'd picked the wrong sizes.

The clothes had already been so picked over we had to compromise greatly. And when I say compromise greatly, I mean no one got what they wanted. The boy who wanted a minion shirt got a Jurassic Park one instead. The boy who wanted Darth Vader got R2-D2 instead. The boy who wanted Spider-Man got the minion shirt his brother wanted, which provided a fantastic opportunity for a loud chorus of "Aw, no fair!"

By the time we made it to the sock and underwear aisle, I was done caring. The 8-year-old got a pack of boxer briefs a whole size too large, the 6-year-old picked out some socks he'll probably regret choosing the first time he wears shorts and realizes how ridiculous he looks in green and blue stripes that come up to his knees. The 4-year-old picked up a package of socks you needed sunglasses to behold.

Oh, well. Lesson learned. Last time I'll take my kids school shopping with me.

Although, now that I think of it, next year will surely be different, because the boys will be older and more mature, and they'll understand the whole budget thing better and, because of all that, they won't annoy me twelve seconds after we get to the store.

So I guess we'll try again.

How Children Take Care of an Injured Mom

Not long ago I fell down our house stairs and broke my foot.

It's not often that I am sick or injured. I've taken only a handful of sick days in eight years of parenting—because my appendix was about to explode and, after vomiting all night, I thought it was time to have someone take a look at it. The rest of my sick days, I was birthing a human.

As the only female in this household of eight, my boys form quite a force when it comes to taking care of Mama.

They fight over who gets to take the laptop up the stairs so I have a free hand to hold onto the stair rail while carrying the baby. They throw away dirty diapers so I don't have to walk the thirty-seven excruciating steps to the trashcan. They draw me pictures and pick me flowers and leave sweet love notes in the form of sticks ("We brought you a magic wand, Mama!") on my pillow.

I appreciate their help and care. I really do. But, three weeks in, there are, honestly, some things I can do without.

For instance: the constant Shadow following me around, asking me if he can inflate my foot cast. Him, I can do without.

I let him do it once, and now every time I take my cast off to rest my foot on the couch, he gets this excited gleam in his eye, because he knows that, eventually, the cast will have to go back on. He knows that, eventually, the cast will need to be re-inflated, because I will have to walk to the kitchen to fix dinner.

I'm tired of being stalked by the Inflation Predator, son. Thank you for your help. But no thanks.

There's another predator who lurks in the doorway when I'm struggling in and out of the bath.

See, it takes me ten minutes to remove the cast and ease myself into a bath balancing on both hands and one leg, and it takes practice.

So my triceps weren't as strong as I thought they were. So a few times I've slipped. Big deal. I didn't cry out or ask for help or shout curse words like I did when I was falling down the stairs. I mainly laughed hysterically because I didn't die in a bathtub.

I guess this boy thought I was weeping instead of laughing, though, because he's always lingering right outside the door, close enough to hear my every move.

"I'd like to take a bath by myself," I say. "With no one else around."

"I'm just making sure you don't fall," he says.

I appreciate your concern, son. But please. Leave me alone. Let me take a bath in peace.

Then there is the predator who walks behind me on the stairs.

To be fair, all my boys are a little freaked out that Mama, normally so athletic and graceful (HA!), fell down the stairs and broke the second bone she's ever broken in her life (the first was a pinky. I tried to catch a softball with the wrong hand.). Even Husband reminds me, every time I approach the stairs, to be careful and take my time.

But there is one boy affected more than the others, so he has taken to walking one step behind me on my way up the stairs so he can catch me if I fall (as if I don't weigh three times as much as he does and wouldn't flatten him on contact).

This would be all nice and sweet IF he didn't also feel the need to make comments about my appearance as we're walking up the stairs.

"You wore those shorts yesterday, Mama," he says. He laughs. "Did you?" He laughs again. "I think you wore them the day before that, too. Did you, Mama?"

Truth is, I've worn them for four days straight, because they're comfy enough to wear to bed, and I can just roll out and not have to wrestle into new clothes while balancing on one foot.

"What's that blue line on the back of your knee, Mama?" he says.

It's called a varicose vein, baby.

"Why is it there?"

Because I had a lot of children.

"You're really slow, Mama."

Thanks for noticing, baby.

"And your booty is bigger than my face."

Sometimes I think about falling backwards on purpose.

The twins have excused themselves from this "help Mama get better" phase. They actually are working harder to NOT make me well. They leave blankets all over the floor so I can trip over them. They "accidentally" step on the boot. They drop water on the floor without telling anyone so I slip and almost break something else.

The constant questions are another way my boys express concern.

"Is your foot still broken, Mama?" (I hear this a billion times a day.)

No, I just like wearing this good-looking boot.

"Can I wear your boot, Mama?"

Of course, dear. I'm only wearing it because I want to. Also, even though it comes up to your thigh, I'm sure you'll find a way to walk with a stiff leg where others have failed.

"When will you get better?"

Well, kids, that depends a lot on you.

The predators and booby traps and questions can all get pretty annoying, but mostly I'm just glad they care enough to ask about my wellbeing. I'm glad they want to do what they can to help me heal.

Or maybe they're just worried that we'll have tossed salads for dinner indefinitely because I haven't cooked a decent meal since it happened.

On second thought, that's probably exactly what it is.

Ain't Nobody Got Time for a Pinterest Perfect Party

There is this weird thing that happens when you have multiple children.

You only add them one at a time, so you start out so well. Setting up that nursery in old-fashioned airplanes. Displaying books on the dresser so they're all nice and neat and you can see each one. Organizing outings to the park and the pool and the children's museum with all his little infant buddies.

And then you have more children. You start letting things fall through the cracks. You start losing track of time. You start slacking when it comes to things like…birthdays.

Not long ago we celebrated our third son's fifth birthday. I forgot to plan his birthday party.

So I scheduled it for two weeks after his actual birth day and then had to listen to him every single morning say, "Well, I guess I'm not having a birthday party this year" after I answered the initial, "Is TODAY my birthday party?" with a negative. If only 5-year-olds weren't so bad at time relativity.

"Your birthday party isn't *today*," I'd say. "It's in another ten days."

"So tomorrow?"

He can count to one hundred, but he can't count the ten days between the day he asked and the day with the box that says "BIRTHDAY PARTY" in big blue letters on the calendar beside the fridge.

One day he took the guilt a little farther. "I didn't get a cupcake for breakfast on my birthday," he said.

It's tradition in our house that the birthday boy gets a cupcake for breakfast on his actual birth day. He got cinnamon toast this year, because I'm ~~drowning~~ doing just fine.

"But you had cinnamon toast," I said. He looked at me like he was the most neglected boy in the world.

"We'll plan what we're having for your birthday party tonight," I said. "How about that?"

He perked up. "How much longer until after dinner?" he said.

We ate our dinner, did all the chores, and then sat down at the table to plan. I had my pen and notebook at the ready.

"What theme do you want?" Husband asked.

"What's a theme?" our 5-year-old said.

"Like Robin Hood or Treasure Island or Star Wars," our 8-year-old bookworm said.

"I want Penguins of Madagascar with ninjas," the birthday-boy-for-the-last-week said.

Husband and I looked at each other with the same "What the—" expression on our faces. But I knew there was a solution. We live in an artsy fartsy world, after all.

I opened Pinterest.

What a mistake.

Now, I used to be a pretty crafty person. When my 8-year-old started school, I sent him there with five reusable napkins and five handkerchiefs complete with a monogrammed picture drawn by all the members of his family so he wouldn't feel lonely during the school day. I know. I'm an overachiever. But no longer. When the next-in-line started school, he was lucky to get two of each. The third starts in a little more than three weeks. I've done all of zero.

My closet is full of material I always intended to use for on-the-go crayon bags and custom backpacks and notebook covers. There are baskets filled with ripped-up books I plan on using for craft projects someday (I've been waiting three years for someday. So far.). I have a bag that sits beside the living room couch for when the kids are all serenely playing and I can take out that blanket I've been crocheting for five years (I haven't touched the blanket, because boys hardly ever serenely play).

But the feed for a "Penguins of Madagascar party" was crazy. Homemade cakes with 3D penguins made from icing, standing up on top. Elaborate crafts that we could have for all the kids at the party (and who would clean up the mess? Me.). Coloring pages and games and party favors with penguins hand-drawn on the sides of cups.

I scrolled through. Can't do this. Can't do this. Won't do this.

Shouldn't have even looked.

When the oldest boy had his Star Wars party last year, I made Ham Solo sandwiches and Wookie cookies and Yoda soda. This year I just wanted to bake chocolate cookies and call them bombs.

I felt a little guilty about it. I couldn't help it.

We live in such a Pinterest-perfect world. People post those elaborate cakes where 3D characters from The Jungle Book are standing up on a no-lines-in-the-icing cake, striking their elaborate pounce poses, and I wonder how anyone plans a birthday anymore with pressure like this.

"Think you could do this?" I asked Husband, pointing to an

impressive cake, because he's the artist.

"Absolutely not," he said. "Who has time for that?"

Exactly. Who has time for that? Last time we tried to decorate a cake in the kitchen, the 8-year-old tried to walk up stairs in roller blades and Spider-Man's mask came out looking more like a face behind bars. Last time we tried to make our own pin-the-mustache-on-the-Lorax game, a little brother found some scissors and cut up all the school papers left in the basket beside the table. Last time we tried to make those hand-lettered food labels the twins discovered the plunger and a toilet their brothers forgot to flush.

So it's not a party unless it's a Pinterest party? Unless we spend two whole days making sure everything is perfect? Unless someone can tell us what that blob on the cake is supposed to be?

No thanks.

Pinterest can go take a walk all the way to Antarctica. Hey, Pinterest: Don't let the ice numb your backside on the way out.

I'll take my imperfect party with the rowdy kids and the penguin box game we never finished and the cake balls we called eggs any day.

See, the thing is, our kids have no idea. They have *no idea*. They hardly notice the clothes they took off and left all over the floor or the shoes they pretty much ran right out of or the way they smell when they come back in from playing outside in the middle of a Texas summer. Do we really think they're gong to notice the way the eyes on that penguin-that-doesn't-really-look-like-a-penguin are lopsided? Do we really think they're going to say there just weren't enough decorations at their party? Do we really think they're going to point out the way the cake sinks in the middle?

No. They're going to shove that cake in their pie holes. We should, too (well, maybe use a fork), because it's dang delicious.

When my son's party was over, I pulled him close and asked him if he enjoyed it.

"Oh, yeah," he said. "It was the best party ever."

And he meant it.

He started to run off and then turned back around. "Can I have another poop cupcake, Mama?" he said.

"Poop cupcake?" I said. "That doesn't sound very tasty."

I thought he was joking, because, well, boys and jokes. The grosser the better. But my boy was dead serious. He pointed to two cupcakes left on the table, each with chocolate icing swirled up high.

I laughed so hard I cried.

Guess those pretty cupcakes weren't as pretty as I thought.

What an Anniversary Looks Like with Kids

Husband and I recently celebrated our anniversary. With the kids.

Most years we try to get at least a couple of days away from the kids so that we can enjoy a little one-on-one time and actually finish conversations instead of keeping them running throughout a whole day to pick back up in the spaces where kids aren't talking, which is hardly ever. Actually it's never, so you have conversations in your heads and forget it was all imaginary and then you get mad at each other when it's time to go to that school meeting you talked about earlier this week and one of you didn't remember. Because the conversation never happened. You just thought it did.

But this year our anniversary fell on a weekend when my parents could not take the children, because they live in a small town, and they were having a bake sale where my mom, the town library director, was expected to make an appearance. She couldn't juggle six kids while trying to sell brownies. I don't blame her. That would be a losing battle, unless she wanted to buy all the brownies.

So after we put the kids to bed on Saturday night, we watched an episode of Game of Thrones, season two (I know we're way behind. Watching something together is like having a conversation together —it hardly ever happens, except in your imagination.). And then we were so tired we just went to bed at a wimpy 10 p.m. instead of the typical Friday night's midnight hour—and it's a good thing we did, because the 3-year-old twins decided, at 4 a.m., that they were going to climb over the baby gate barring their room for sanity purposes and go exploring the library unsupervised, which is always a frightening proposition with twins.

Our home library is right outside our bedroom, and we totally would have heard their pounding footsteps and victory-cry screeching if Husband hadn't turned up the "storm sounds" white noise on the computer so we could get some sleep by pretending there were no kids in the house. So the 8-year-old took it upon himself to knock on our door and let us know his brothers were "running wild in the library."

They weren't in there for long, but already one of them had eaten nearly a whole tube of toothpaste that he climbed a cabinet in the bathroom to get and emptied out a bottle of essential oil Husband had left next to a diffuser. His whole mouth smelled like Peace & Calming with some strawberry thrown in like an afterthought. So we took Strawberry Shortcake back to bed, along with his probably-not-innocent-either-but-we-couldn't-find-any-evidence-of-twinanigans brother and closed their door, which has a lock on the outside (because twins. That's all I'm going to say. You can judge if you want. I don't care. Because twins.).

Husband and I really wanted to go back to sleep, because we still had two more hours until we needed to be up to get everyone ready for church, but the problem was, the shrieking banshees who had been set loose in the library minutes before had already woken the rest of the boys. We told them to read in the library for the next two hours, because they love to read and we love to sleep.

When we woke up at 7, everyone was crying. The 8-year-old was crying because he was starving, and he was going to die if he didn't get anything to eat RIGHT THIS MINUTE. The 6-year-old was crying because his older brother, in a fit of anger, had taken a book right out of his hands. The 5-year-old was crying because he's 5 and that's enough explanation in his mind. The 3-year-olds were crying because they were up at 4. The baby was crying because he heard all his brothers crying, and he decided he should probably be crying, too.

We explained to everyone that it was our anniversary and they should be the ones fixing us breakfast, but no one seemed to like that idea, so Husband went downstairs to cook a feast of toast with jam, while I showered and put on a little makeup, because I'm not a big fan of scaring church people away with my nakedness. Naked face, that is. Geez. The words aren't coming out right. I've been up since 4.

And then we left for church half an hour late and blissfully handed the boys off to the nursery workers and Sunday school teachers, not saying a word about how they'd probably be really grouchy because everyone had been up since 4, and then we went out with the baby into the service. Two minutes in, the baby started happily shrieking in the middle of the pastor's talk, so all the heads (smiling mostly) turned toward me while I tried to gracefully exit the row and, in typical Rachel fashion, tripped over some chairs and nearly crapped my pants because I didn't want to drop the baby. This story has a happy ending, because I didn't drop the baby or crap my pants. But I did end up with a busted-up knee. Much better than a busted-up baby or a pair of smelly drawers.

Baby and I danced in the entry-way of the church while I counted down the minutes until the boys would be ours again.

When we got back home, the house was a wreck, because the day before we'd taken everybody to the city zoo and Husband and I didn't feel like enforcing any of the normal cleanup rules when we got back home, because six kids out at the zoo depletes a parent's energy stores for a whole forty-eight hours. So after we wrestled every crayon we own—about a billion—out of the twins' hands and put them down for their naps, the 8-year-old found his way to our room and said, "Because it's your anniversary, I'll do whatever you want me to do for you today. And the rest of this week, too."

Which was sweet and all, except "whatever you want me to do for you" doesn't actually mean whatever you want me to do for you, because I asked him to cook dinner, and he said that probably wouldn't be safe, which is probably true, and then I asked him to watch his brothers so his daddy and I could go for a walk around the cul-de-sac, and he said he could do anything but watching his brothers and cooking dinner, and then I asked him to clean up his room because it was a mess, and he said he would do anything *for me*, and cleaning his room wasn't *for me*, so I just gave up after that.

We cooked our dinner of pasta in Vodka sauce and sat around the table telling stories about the early days before Husband and I were married, while the kids listened with silly grins on their faces, because what's better than watching a mama and daddy who love each other tell stories about how they came to be?

And after all that we put them all to bed so we could stuff our faces with the salted caramel cupcakes we'd hidden in the pantry.

It was divine. Truly. Best anniversary ever. Except for the one where we ditched the kids and went to Disney World. But this one was a very distant second.

The Best Humble-Bragging Christmas Card Ever

Merry Christmas!

I know that you all are secretly wanting to hear from me about my truly exceptional kids, so I decided that this year, instead of a card, I would just send out a Christmas newsletter so I could humble-brag about these boys who really are the most amazing kids ever. I hope you stick around to see how much better I think my kids are than yours.

The family

First, I really have to commend our family. We have left the house three hundred thirty-four times this year, and we have only been late three hundred twenty-six of those. This is quite an accomplishment, believe me. We really are extraordinary. When you can leave the house on time EVEN THOUGH someone decides at the last minute that he needs to go to the potty and then he overflows the toilet, or another one decides he left something critically important in his room and now can't find it under the massive mountains of clothes he didn't put away last laundry day, or, God forbid, fifteen of the left shoes are missing, you have made it. You really have.

The 9-year-old

This boy has only had his behavior folder marked "transition trouble" seventy-nine of the eighty days he's been in school, and he's been late to school ONLY sixteen times. Something to be proud of, I know. Just this morning he threw his fourteenth LEGO creation in anger, because he couldn't find the right "brown brick" piece, and "it would be totally ruined without the brown brick piece." He has "accidentally" broken three pieces of furniture this year by turning flips on it even though he's twice as big as he used to be back when it was okay.

He's also learned all of three songs on the piano (taught himself!!!) and plays them incessantly so we've all started changing the lyrics for "Pass the Pumpkin All Around" to "God, I really hate this song. I don't want to sing along, Oooooh, oooooh, let it stop at you." We are thoroughly proud of this boy, who prefers reading a book to listening to instructions, which makes our house really fun and easy.

The 6-year-old

This boy created a special dance move called "The Hipster," which is really just a hip thrust with a little bouncing thrown in. I'm pretty sure Elvis Presley might have invented it first, but, you know, we want him to believe he's unique and special. And he is the admiration of the family when he busts this move. He also started washing the dishes with the dish wand and has only broken five plates this year. A great start to a great dishwashing career, if you ask me. (One of his Christmas presents is going to be a collection of new plates. Don't tell him!!!)

He has also asked the "How did I get out of your uterus" question twelve times this year and always forgets the answer. Something about it makes it hard to remember. I don't know. Maybe it's some Freudian coping mechanism, like "Don't think about that horrible, jarring, pitch-black passage into the world." If you do happen to ask and he does happen to remember, he'll most likely answer "A Fa China passage." Because we believe in teaching kids biology and the proper names for body parts.

The 5-year-old

This little boy started kindergarten this year, and every single morning (never fails!), he manages to misplace his shoes. It is really quite a mystery. He has somehow mastered the art of not seeing what's right in front of his face, which, as you can imagine, is a fantastic quality to have. It doesn't make the morning get-to-school routine any harder to have to drop everything and "find" the shoes that are right beside his feet because he "already looked and can't find them." He has also, somehow, managed to lose every shoe of one foot and now walks around with only a left foot. You try it and see if you don't trip. I'm telling you. Exceptional.

He has also phonetically learned how to spell words like his countrified Nonny says them—sol for saw, mayen for man, mayilk for milk.

3-year-old number 1

Twin 1 has had quite a year. He has ruined fifteen pairs of pants by expertly scooting around on his knees, no matter how many times he's been told not to do exactly that (great initiative!). He has also ruined four pairs of shoes, because he forgot he left them in the backyard. They got baked in the sun, and now we have four pairs of tie-dyed Converse sneakers. I'm actually super impressed that he learned how to tie dye without even trying. I remember that being a really complicated thing back when I was in elementary school.

This one has also put his shoes on the wrong feet three hundred sixty-four times this year, which has added exactly two minutes and fifteen seconds to our morning routine (not counting the five minutes and twenty-three seconds of arguing about it—"This IS the right foot, Mama." "No it's not, buddy." "YES IT IS!" "Trust me." "IT IS THE RIGHT FOOT!" [four minutes of the same.] "Okay. Try to walk in them."). Of the other accomplishments, this is probably the most notable: He learned how to open a gummy vitamin bottle and consumed the entire contents while I was otherwise occupied by a massive blowout diaper, courtesy of his baby brother. He's never had so much diarrhea before. I know! Another accomplishment for the baby book!

3-year-old number 2

Twin 2 nearly contracted a bacterial infection three times from unauthorized play with the plunger. He can't help but take this charming toy for a test drive, if it happens to be anywhere near a toilet. Left alone in the bathroom for five seconds? I think I'll plunge the toilet. Mama's watching? Brother will distract her while I plunge it. Mama's upstairs dumping the laundry on the bed? I WILL PLUNGE IT! This typically happens when the toilet water is brown with the most delightful presents, and he proficiently sloshes said water all over the walls. It is quite lovely, as I'm sure you can imagine. Part of his Christmas present will pay for a cleaning service that will dare to touch those walls.

This little boy also figured out how to make gigantic spitballs out of toilet paper rolls and actually get them to stick to the walls and ceiling. He will soon be featured in the Guinness Book of World Records for "Most Annoying 3-year-old."

The baby

This little guy. He has not thrown up all over himself today, which is quite a feat. This year he also put twenty-seven Happy Baby organic kale and spinach puffs in his right ear before finally, thankfully, mastering the art of feeding himself. He's only had one major poop blowout, which is saying a whole lot for a Toalson baby.

He also has managed to eat some really impressive things that are ground into our carpet—three-day-old bread, wads of hair, possibly a toenail, old toilet paper that was stuck to someone's shoe, and a dozen other unclassifiable objects. In a dramatic turn of irony, he's the only one of us who bypassed the vomit-rocket virus this year, which means he's likely the healthiest among us. It's a great case for eating whatever you find on the floor. Or not.

Other random accomplishments

The older three boys are quite gifted in the art of armpit farts. I bet we could even fart "We Wish You A Merry Christmas," complete with two harmonies, but we're saving that for our Christmas card next year.

I'm sure you can see why I'm so proud of my brilliant boys. But the real reason I'm telling you all this is to show you that Husband and I really rocked our parenting this year. We only yelled two hundred fifty-seven times, and we only said, "I tap out" every other day, and we only complained about the maddening things our kids do for about four hours of every day. That's saying a whole lot, and I think we deserve a congratulations!

I hope you have a wonderful holiday with your not-as-exceptional-as-mine family. And may your new year be as noteworthy as my old year was.

Let's Get Serious For a Minute

Unsolicited Advice Can Take This Job and Shove It

I just have to say it: I'm not a big fan of unsolicited parenting advice.

I believe in seeking wisdom for our parenting journey (because who of us really knows what we're doing?) by reading parenting books or parenting articles or talking with friends who have walked in our shoes, and I do all of that. But it seems like being pregnant or becoming a brand new mom or rising through the ranks of a toddler parent or adolescent parent or teenager parent suddenly gives people permission (because they've already raised their kids or they're in a stage above yours or they think they know all there is to know about parenting) to tell you how to raise your children.

Maybe it's because most of the unsolicited advice I've gotten has been contrary to the way I know is right for my children, or maybe it's because most of the people who have doled out that advice have done it just to say I'm doing it all wrong, but I don't often heed what people say when I've never asked for their advice in the first place.

Just to be clear, I'm not talking about the friend you talk to most every day or the ones you swap parenting battle stories with or the ones who hold multiple degrees in child development or work as child therapists or are experts in parenting with respect and teaching children emotional intelligence (I'll take unsolicited advice from you any day!).

I'm talking about the lady who watches your son melt down at the playground because it's time to go and he's not ready to go, the one who cuts her eyes at you and says, "What that boy really needs is some discipline," and what she really means is a good old-fashioned spanking.

I'm talking about the one who thinks that because "cry it out" worked for her three children, who are grown with no psychological problems, it will most definitely work for yours, too, because people who soothe instead of let babies "cry it out" are really just spoiling their children, and later on those children will be ill-equipped to face this unfair world and you'll regret you ever picked them up to soothe them, because that was the time they could have learned all about life not being fair. When they were infants.

I'm talking about all the others who believe they raised their children right and good and proper, even though those children were never *your* children.

So, since we seem to live in this age where people believe "the village" of "it takes a village to raise a child" means they are given unauthorized permission to weigh in (without being asked) on how the world's parents raise their children, I wanted to highlight the unsolicited (and solicited) parenting advice I find the most helpful and give us all permission to toss the rest.

1. It makes me a better parent.

The advice that is valuable to me equips me with practical tools to help me understand my children in their various developmental stages and encourages me to mold their personalities and temperaments and tendencies not in a way that is easiest for me but in a way that is the best representation of who they were made to be.

2. It honors and embraces who children are.

One of the most important pieces of parenting advice that I've gotten in all my soliciting (never the unsolicited, unfortunately) is to accept who my children are already. It's not easy, when one is strong-willed and it would be easier if he weren't; and one is highly sensitive and cries about the least little thing, and it would be easier if he weren't; and one is active and daring and full of courage, and it would be easier if he weren't; and one wants to do everything for himself even though he's only 2, and it would be easier if he didn't; and one is afraid of the dark and wants to sleep in the doorway instead of his bed, and it would be easier if he didn't.

The most helpful advice encourages me to honor who my children are instead of telling me how I should be changing them into more acceptable people.

3. It fills me with a sense of empowerment, not inefficiency.

So much of the unsolicited advice these days is given in a way that makes parents feel like we're failing as parents, just because we're not doing it this one particular way that works for all children of all ages at all times. The best parenting advice acknowledges that every child is different and that I, as a parent, know my child best and already possess the ability to raise them right.

4. It doesn't throw out terms like "entitled" or "helicopter" or "spoiled" or "they have to learn life isn't fair."

These are old-fashioned terms that really have no applicable value whatsoever. They've been used since before the turn of the 20th century. They're well past retirement age.

5. It doesn't make assumptions about who parents are.

So much of today's parenting advice, especially the unsolicited kind, comes from people who don't really know our family or our children, who only see them every other month or on birthdays or at the store that one time our kid had their meltdown because it was 1 p.m. and he hadn't had anything to eat or drink since 8 a.m.

The other day I was checking out at the store with one boy loudly crying that he wanted to spend more time than I allowed looking at the toys and two other boys physically fighting over who got to fly like Superman on the bottom rack of the cart.

The woman checking me out handed me my receipt and caught my eye and smiled.

"Three boys is such a blessing," she said.

I didn't tell her that there were three more at home driving their daddy crazy or that, look, my boys were fighting or that they sure don't always act like a blessing.

I just smiled back and said, "Yes. They are," and then walked out the door with my blessings still crying and fighting.

Sometimes the best unsolicited advice is just a reminder that these little people really are amazing.

The rest of it, well, we can just let it slide in one ear and right back out the other, smiling our brightest thank-you smile. They don't have to know we weren't listening.

The Splendor of the 2 a.m. Feeding

It's quiet, and it's dark, and it's only you and me.

All day long your brothers have pulled and demanded and captured my time while you have slept and dreamed and grown, little by little by little. But right now is our time, because brothers are sleeping and Daddy is snoring beside us and the whole world is silently breathing its way toward morning.

And it doesn't matter that I'm so exhausted or that I will wake again in three hours to start the morning whirlwind of a school day. It only matters that you are here with me, that you are looking at me with those eyes that just might stay blue this time, that I can kiss a tiny face back into sleep once a belly is full.

It doesn't matter that all day I have poured milk for your brothers and cooked breakfasts and lunches and cleaned up after dinner, that I will do it all again in too little time. It only matters that there is this quiet, still moment when I get to hold you and only you, when I get to talk softly to you and only you, when I get to stare at you and only you.

Your brothers, they used to be you once, and I know exactly how this will go, because they used to enjoy the holding and the talking and the kissing and the staring, and now they are too big for laps and too busy for talking and too old for kissing and staring.

This will go fast and sharp and bittersweet.

So I will have you to myself, for this one moment in time.

I bend to kiss you, and it is overwhelming, the love that cracks a whole heart wide open, again, because you are tiny, and you are last, and you are only thirteen days old. I bend to kiss you again, and it is overwhelming, the sadness, because you are tiny, and you are last, and I know your peaceful sleep in my arms won't last forever. Not even close.

So I will take time where I can—and here it is, in the dark of early morning, when everyone else sleeps and you meet me, for the thirteenth time. I hold you close, longer that I would if I were concerned about sleep, longer than I would if I were thinking of the day ahead and all the challenges it will likely hold.

Because this is our time, you and me.

So what the clock tells me makes no difference whatsoever, because we are together, and this time belongs to you. Only you. This time is frozen. Sacred. Beautiful. It widens the heart of a mama so another little boy can take his seat inside.

I drink every moment, every breath, every flicker of a smile, every stretch. I watch you feed, touching the soft skin of your cheek, feeling the weight of you in the crook of my arm, memorizing the curve of that nose and the flutter of an eye that blinks open and shut again beneath the soft glow of a lamp.

I gaze and soak and adore, oblivious to time's ticking, because some things transcend time.

Like a 2 a.m. feeding.

And when you are done, when I am done, I kiss your face once more and wrap my arms just a little tighter, and then I fold the blanket around your still-tiny-for-today body and put you back to sleep, whispering the words I always whisper when our time has met its end.

See you at 2 a.m., my love.

Ready or Not, Time Marches Ever On

This weekend I opened whole boxes of emotion.

I sat in a living room, sorting through all the clothes my boys wore as babies, washing them and hanging them and breathing them, and I arranged all those tiny unnecessary shoes into rows so they would be ready for this last baby of mine who will come any day now.

I pulled out the red outfit, the one my firstborn wore the night he first laughed, a sound I'll never, ever forget, even though it's been eight years. I found the shirt my second-in-line was wearing when he first gifted the smile that still melts my heart today. I showed their daddy the white shirt, now stained irreparably, the third was wearing when he first walked out of his room on two feet instead of the four he used to bear-crawl his way around.

First Christmas, first swim day, first day home from the hospital. It's amazing how many memories those clothes hold, how they mark time more surely than we can in our everyday lives.

Was he ever really this small, eight pounds instead of fifty-eight pounds? How could these tiny swim trucks have fit the boy with legs long enough to put him level with my chest? How did that tiny baby become the one who graduates to the big boy side of the store in just a few months?

Where did the time go?

I tried not to cry, looking at all those clothes, remembering, but I am a mama.

These years of raising babies and toddlers and almost-adolescents make the days seem so long, but the years are incredibly short. Before we even know it, before we're really even ready, they come up to our shoulders and they weigh fifty-eight pounds and they don't need us like they used to.

Time to grow up.

Time to be their own people.

Time to let them fly.

It's not easy, as a mother, to watch time slipping, because I can still feel their baby weight in my arms, and I can still see their eyes that would look upon a new world but first sought only mine, and I can still hear the babble of their baby talk. And yet now they dress themselves and brush their own teeth and buckle their own seat belts?

Time marched on, and it did not look back.

So often, in these days of great demand and need, when I walk most days with my head spinning, I just put one foot in front of the other, trying to make it to nap time so I have a few hours to finally breathe, and then I'm trying to make it to bedtime so I can finally get some rest to start it all over again tomorrow.

And in my surviving, I'm missing the beauty of a moment right here in front of me.

What will they remember of this childhood I have given them? Will they remember their mama hurrying from one thing to the next thing and never stopping to watch the way that chair makes a perfect curvy track for Lightning McQueen, or will they remember the way I stopped and watched until he was all the way to the table-mountain above the chair-back track?

Will they remember my apologetic dismissal when they want to tell me a story I know, from experience, will take them forty-five minutes to finish, or will they remember that I stopped and looked them in the eye and listened like their words meant the world to me, even though the dryer just went off and if I don't keep those clothes moving, I'll never get the nine loads finished today?

Will they remember the way I yelled those times I was exhausted and overwhelmed and not quite myself, or will they remember the way I loved them in my words and my tone and my actions?

Time is not always a friend, because it tells the truth of our lives, how we wanted to take that camping trip together, but there was never any time; how we thought we'd start playing kickball in the cul-de-sac together, but we ran out of time; how we always planned to make that Christmas video together, year after year after year, but, well, time.

But time is also a forgiver. Time offers a hundred chances for us to get it right.

And so, when we pick up our boys, all wild and crazy from a weekend with the grandparents, I seize time like I seize them, and I gift them with whole presence.

The only gift that really matters.

The only gift that marches in step with time.

To My Obstetrician: Thank You For Delivering These New Lives

Dear Dr. Brougher,

I miss you when I'm not pregnant.

I know it sounds a little crazy. You, the doctor whom every woman dreads that one time a year, because there are stirrups and cold metal and paper-thin sheets to cover everything and nothing at all, but I mean it. I really do.

This last time around, when I learned there would be another baby, part of my excitement was that I would be able to see you again, that you would share, once more, in the most joyous, scary, beautiful moment that can happen in the lives of a man and a woman.

I wonder if you know just what you have done.

The first time I met you, I was three months married, coming in on the recommendation of a friend. You sat me down in your office and told me you'd been a former journalist, because I was one, too. It was the beginning of a friendship.

I asked you all sorts of questions about sex, the ones I'd never been able to ask my mother, and you answered them all in that direct, no-nonsense way of yours. And then you sent me off with a "See you next year," and you did see me the next year and also four months after that, when I took my first pregnancy test and it said yes. You may not know it, but I drove one hundred fifteen miles to see you for that first appointment, because even though we'd moved to another town, I couldn't imagine anyone else delivering my first.

And it's a good thing, too, because there I was in the hospital, three hours pushing and no baby, and when my eyeballs felt like they might explode from the brutal strain, you told me you needed to use a vacuum to get him out.

I went crazy. I cried about how a friend who was a nurse in neonatal intensive care had seen so many cases of brain damage because of the vacuum. "Just don't let them use a vacuum," she'd said two days before I lay on a bed in labor.

You did not laugh at my fear. You took it and held it gently. "That has not been my experience," you said. "But it's entirely up to you."

Those contractions kept coming so I had to scream out, "Whatever you need to do, just get him out," and you did, and he was fine, and you slipped out of that birthing room quietly, because a new mama and daddy were having the moment you've seen a thousand times, and the last thing you wanted to do was intrude. We didn't even have a chance to thank you.

We would have more chances, though.

You would be my rock that this-is-the-safe-day when you ran the wand across my belly and there was no heartbeat, the same day you would deliver a baby and instead of placing her in a new mama's arms you would place her in a lab jar.

You would walk us through a twin pregnancy, a high-risk, share-the-placenta case that has more pages of what could go wrong than what could go right.

You carried me through this last one, and maybe this is the most significant of all.

You see, I didn't know if he would make it. There was that pregnancy condition, when I itched all over day and night. The condition that made me want to scratch my eyes out. The condition that could end in stillbirth.

And, God, I couldn't do that again. I couldn't lose another one.

I cried after every appointment near the end. I had anxiety attacks when he stopped moving for a minute or two. I had dreams about a baby whose face I would not kiss alive.

I sent you notes. I begged you to deliver early, since I'd read all about those stillbirth chances and how they increased the longer babies lived in a womb. I became the patient no obstetrician wants.

And then, the day before my birthday you gave me a gift. A baby, and he was ALIVE.

I love you for that.

I just had my last post-pregnancy appointment with you, because this boy was always going to be our last, and you don't know it, but I felt all torn up inside. Because the truth is I will miss you.

I will miss your humor. I will miss our talks. I will miss sharing in this new life experience with you.

I don't even know that words can express how grateful I am to and for you, but I will try.

Thank you for all you have done.

You saw the fear in my eyes for that first one, and you spoke courage and peace and wisdom. You knew the sorrow of that lost one, and you spoke comfort and hope and healing. You knew the fear and worry that can consume a mama when stillbirth looms, and you spoke calm and understanding and love.

This cannot be underestimated.

Maybe it's not what typical doctors do, this caring enough about a patient to ask about the lost job and the writing pursuit and the husband at home, whose name you remember, but you were never typical.

You were exceptional.

Not only did you deliver new life into the world, but you delivered new life into the heart of this mama, who did not know if she could really do it, any of it.

I will not be the same because of you. My family will not be the same. We are forever changed.

So thank you. Thank you for your gift of life. Thank you for sacrificing weekends so you could deliver every one of my half-dozen boys. Thank you for your love and care and constant concern.

You are a healer in every sense of the word.

The Thing About Mom Guilt

This week Husband and I attended a creative conference in Georgia. The baby was too young to stay with family or friends, so we took him with us.

Every time I had to feed him, I hid out in the bathroom. I made his bottle while hunched in a bathroom stall so I didn't have to share my shame.

You see, I don't breastfeed my baby. I didn't breastfeed any of them.

It's not because I don't want to. God knows I tried every time. I did everything those lactation consultants told me to try with the first one, who ended up in the emergency room two days after we brought him home because he was dehydrated.

Sometimes I wonder if his first few days, the nursing that wasn't really nursing because there wasn't any milk, is why he struggles with anxiety today. Did it change something in his brain, that dehydration? Did it make him feel insecure when he couldn't get enough food? Did it harm him in ways we couldn't even see at the time?

This kind of thinking can drive a mama crazy.

The truth is, I am one of a minority of women who just can't produce enough milk for their babies.

I knew it would happen this time, too. I waited for all the familiar signs, and they came around the same time they had for all the others—about three weeks in. I thought I'd taken the pressure off this time, but no. I didn't. It felt like failure all over again.

That guilt comes creeping in slowly, when another mother asks me how breastfeeding is going and I have to explain why I can't and wonder if she believes me. When I read a new study that finds yet another benefit of breast over bottle. When I am in the presence of other people who may or may not care how I feed my baby.

The publicity around breastfeeding has been great and wonderful and so very helpful for most mothers. It has also been hard for women like me. Mom guilt likes to hide in statistics. It likes to use facts. It likes to twist something beautiful into something dark and ugly.

We moms aren't always the kindest to ourselves, and that mom guilt can come out swinging, and it's vicious and unrelenting and overflowing with shame.

Shame locks us in a bathroom stall so we can try to hide our I-don't-breastfeed secret. It closes us in a house so we can try to hide our I-don't-think-I-like-my-children secret. It steals the courage to venture out to a park or a grocery store or a restaurant so we can try to hide our I-yell-at-my-children secret.

This mom guilt lobs its lies at all the weak places.

You should have handled that more calmly.

You should have spent more time with her.

You should have let him sleep with you.

You should have bought her that toy.

You should have hugged him good night.

You should have built that LEGO house with him.

You should have colored that picture with him when he asked.

You should have cooked a healthy meal instead of ordering in pizza.

You should have planned a better birthday party.

You should have done more.

You should have tried harder.

You should have been better.

Where does it end?

It ends at a mom saying enough is enough.

It ends at moms sharing their secrets. It ends at admitting our fears—that we are afraid our baby won't be as smart because we can't breastfeed; or we're afraid we don't really love that difficult one because he's, well, difficult; or we're afraid no one else has ever dealt with this or felt this way before, because no one ever talks about these hard places so we all just keep pretending they don't exist.

We will never crawl out from beneath the weight of mom guilt if we don't bare ourselves.

Shame cannot get a foothold in the light. Only in the dark.

I don't want to hide in a bathroom stall to make my baby's bottle anymore just because I'm ashamed of my inability to produce milk. I don't want to pretend that I always like my children and that I exact perfect patience in the discipline areas and that I keep a level head at all times. I don't want to wonder if I could have done more or tried harder or been a better mom to my children.

Enough is enough.

We will never know enough or do enough or be enough, at least not according to those ridiculous expectations we put on ourselves. We must choose to believe that we are already enough. We must choose to get real. We must choose to find other mothers who are ready to get real, not the ones who pretend they're perfect.

There is no perfect. There is only good enough.

The thing about mom guilt is that it's only true when we are alone. It's only true if we are hiding. It's only true if we refuse to acknowledge that we will never, ever be perfect.

Sometimes I yell at my children, because I'm just SO ANGRY at them for doing what they're not supposed to do. Sometimes I check out of conversations with my kids because their stories have so many words. Sometimes I wonder if I was out of my mind to have so many.

There. I said it. I feel so much better now.

I'm Just Saying Is All

Just Because I Have a Large Family Doesn't Mean I Didn't Family Plan

I'm sitting in a chair, waiting to do an interview for my job, when she walks through the door, this woman I haven't seen in eight months but have known for years, and she looks at me and drops her mouth and says, "Oh my God. Don't tell me you're pregnant again."

It's pretty obvious that my six-months swelling belly is not the bloating of a meal gone wrong.

I just smile and wait for the words I know will come, and she doesn't disappoint me.

"Don't you know by now how this happens?" she says.

No, I don't. Would you please enlighten me? Because, good Lord, who wants six accidents like I've got?

That's what I want to say. I don't, of course.

I usually try to take these comments with good humor and lots and lots of patience, because I know people are just trying to say something, and they think it's funny. They don't know how many times I've heard it before.

But now that we are entrenched in our fifth pregnancy, the comments happen nearly every encounter I have with someone I haven't seen in a while.

"You're pregnant every time I see you," someone else says today, and I can only shake my head and flash my obligatory smile and wait for the next punch.

And it comes, like I suspected it would, from a guy who flippantly remarks, "Yeah, my wife and I believe in family planning."

It's this misconception right here that makes me want to scream it from the rooftops: Just because we have a large family doesn't mean we didn't family plan.

Sure, maybe we didn't plan in the "traditional" ways, with birth control pills and rings and prevent-a pregnancy cups, but there are other ways to family plan—like counting days and taking temperatures and being careful. It may be news to many, but every one of our six babies was planned (Okay, okay, we didn't plan for the extra twin.).

I know it's hard to believe that a family in our day and age and a society like this one would choose to have six children, and maybe it seems a little crazy (it is) and wildly expensive (yes), but we did. And even though there are days I wonder if we really *were* crazy, and I shudder to think about our grocery bill in a few years, and I cringe beneath the insensitive comments of other people, I wouldn't change a thing about our lives.

I used to be one of the most annoying control freaks a person could ever be. I used to think a clean and tidy house was a non-negotiable. I used to walk through life distracted to the best parts—all those tiny little pieces I needed a child to show me.

Now I'm the mama who can't keep up with school paperwork and says *oh well*, and I'm the mama paying library fines every few weeks, and I'm the mama stepping over a discarded shoe and laughing about how this one is here and the other is clear across the room, balancing on the edge of a couch top, and how in the world did that happen?

Now I'm the mama who will slide down stairs in an oversized box just for a laugh from my boys, even though I almost break my back in the process. I'm the mama who laughs myself silly at an ABC song boys recorded with their daddy and turned slow motion. I'm the mama who stops on the walk to school so we can observe the ways those squished earthworms look like a J and an L and an S and an E, and who cares if we're late?

I like this person I've become.

So to all the people who feel the need to comment on how maybe we need to take our hands off each other until we can figure out where babies come from; and the ones who say we sure have a huge family and "better you than me," like having a large family is some kind of curse; and the ones who want to educate us on their ideas about family planning, I say thank you.

Thank you for reminding me just how amazing my nontraditional-according-to-numbers family really is. Thank you for helping me realize more clearly and firmly and surely that this is who I want to be, a mother of six boys, a woman losing a grip on her ordered-just-so life.

Thank you for showing me that this is family planning at its best.

10 Ways My Boys Make Me Fashionably "Green"

Many times, when I mention anywhere in the online world that I'm a mom of six boys, all the amateur environmentalists come out to play, not realizing that I'm actually a closet environmentalist myself. Over the years, I have convinced Husband to trade antibiotics for sustainably harvested essential oils, paper products for dishware (unless we have a lazy Saturday), and toxic cleaning and personal care products for the homemade version (ever seen a man put on deodorant with his bare hands? He does in my house. And smells like lavender, too.). We stopped just short of reusable toilet paper, but not because I wasn't game. That was Husband's line.

My kids have helped us in this becoming-environmentally-friendly pursuit, in ways that have astonished me over the years. I never would have thought of these simple ways to save the earth.

1. If it's yellow, let it mellow.

They don't flush the toilet. Like hardly ever. You might lift a lid and get a heat wave of urine right in your face (or worse, if you're really lucky—which it turns out I am every single day). If I want to use a bathroom, I better be using my own, because theirs has been mellowing for days. And it smells exactly like a dead animal rotting in a swamp.

Saves on: Water and wastewater.

2. Bath water can be consumed.

That's right. Bath time is not only wash time. It's also hydration time, because they'll fill up the bath cup that's supposed to be used to wash off the eco-friendly soap in their hair, and they'll drink that nastiness instead, no matter how many times I've told them it's gross. (So gross. Do you know how dirty you are?) Also, if one brother has already finished his bath and left the water in the tub, another brother will get in and wash anyway (and still drink the water). And while we're on the subject, I'll admit that their daddy and I only have time for showers every two or three days, so. Winning. (Don't worry. We make our own deodorant, which we apply every morning to convince people that we have it all together. As long as they don't notice my greasy hair.)

Saves on: Water, wastewater, energy.

3. They'll wear the same Iron Man costume with nothing else underneath for four days straight.

Or the same pair of pajamas. Or the same sweat pants. They're not picky at all. They just want to wear what's comfortable. For a week. This saves us the most in the summer, when it's too hot in Texas to wear clothes. They just run around in their ~~underwear~~ swim trunks instead.

Saves on: Water, wastewater, energy.

4. Paper of any kind is good for drawing.

This means their brother's class list for Valentine's Day is a good place to draw a 2-year-old version of a spider. So is that flier for lawn mowing services and the thousand other pieces of junk mail waiting in our mailbox to clutter up our counter. Might as well put it to good use. Thanks, kids.

Saves on: Paper waste.

5. Sharing is caring.

If one pulls out an organic apple and puts it down, another will find it and finish it. No food is wasted around here. And when they're finished, someone will find that apple core and take it on outside to plant seeds and feed birds. (We're still waiting for those apple trees to start sprouting, but I hear Texas isn't so great for growing apples because it's ten thousand degrees here.)

Saves on: Food waste.

6. They prefer unpackaged foods.

Actually, that's not true. Give them a choice between a chocolate bar and a piece of organic fruit, and they'll take the chocolate bar (unless they ask their parents… in which case they'll take the fruit). But their daddy and I stick to the peripheries of the store, so they don't really have a choice. They'll eat two pounds of organic spinach before they starve.

Saves on: Energy required to package foods, chemicals buried in food and released in air.

7. What's TV?

It's been years since we got rid of cable and threw out the television. Our boys spend their days outside making movies with an old camera or pretending fallen tree branches are light sabers or creating hole-in the-yard art masterpieces their daddy and I will trip in later.

Saves on: Electricity, consumption messages spread through commercials.

8. Weeds are just another word for flowers.

Our boys gather them into a bouquet for Mama. They give them to the neighbor girls. They pick the dandelions and make their wishes. We have no use for herbicides, and guess what? We have the greenest yard on the block. Weird.

Saves on: Chemicals leaching into groundwater.

9. Fertilization is free.

Boys like releasing bodily fluids outside. No, we don't have a dog. That's probably just the accidental waste of our two 2-year-olds (who, by the way, have been told not to number-2-it out in the yard. But, you know, 2-year-olds). It's OK, though. Just watch your step on your way to admiring the prettiest peach and pear trees in the city.

Saves on: Synthetic fertilizers, chemicals leaching into groundwater.

10. Energy is free (and plenty).

We live half a mile from our boys' school. So we walk or ride bikes or race on scooters. A little more than half a mile down the road is the neighborhood park. A mile down the road is a frozen yogurt shop and a pizza place, perfect for the monthly family night out. After walking or running or, most likely, racing to all those places, our boys will still have energy left over. One of these days we'll find a way to bottle it up and patent it for selling. Or just drink it ourselves.

Saves on: gas, emissions from a car.

There are many intentional ways we teach our boys about environmentalism and social justice—because environmentalism always boils down to social justice—but I did not expect our boys to help us along the journey. So I can only say to these six wonderful little people: Thank you. You have made the world a better place in so many ways.

I'm so glad you're here.

The Mysterious (Or Not-So-Mysterious) Phenomenon of Perfect Parents

I used to be a perfect parent. Well, actually, who am I kidding? I still am. Between the hours of 9:30 p.m. and 4:30 a.m.

Unless, of course, one of the kids wakes me up.

The rest of the time, (which is anytime my kids are awake, in case you didn't catch that) I'm a less-than-stellar parent. I hate to admit this, because I really wanted to join the Perfect Parents Club (P.P. from here on out), and I know there will probably be a whole lot of P.P.s out there lamenting the fact that I have six boys who should probably only be trusted to P.P.s.

Well. I remember being one of those. I remember Husband and I would go out to eat before we had kids, and we would see a kid throwing a tantrum, right in the middle of the restaurant floor, and we would look at each, our eyes screaming it if our mouths couldn't. *Never, ever,* they said. *Not in a million years would we let a kid lose his mind like that.* I would meet a stay-at-home mom in her home to interview her for a news story I was working on, and her kid would be climbing all over the back of the couches and her head and the table while his mother was otherwise occupied, and I would leave thinking, *My kid will never be that kid.* I would hear an 8-year-old backtalk his mother, and I would shake my head. *Absolutely not.*

I wish I could laugh in that clueless woman's face.

I had kids. I had a toddler who didn't want to leave the park, so he took off running hyper-speed, screaming bloody murder so people who didn't know I was his mother probably thought I was kidnapping him against his will. I had the boy who thought it would be fun to jump off the upright piano onto the couch and nailed the landing so impressively I was too shocked to even correct him. I had a spirited 8-year-old.

The thing about P.P.s is they either have a really short memory or they don't have kids at all—in which case they should stop talking to the rest of us about our lackluster parenting.

None of us is a P.P. Sometimes we get really lucky with a kid who has an easy-going temperament. I've got two out of the six. The rest of them trade off being devils on an hour-by-hour basis.

It's not because we're bad parents. We're about as perfect as we're probably ever going to be. And that's okay. It's perfectly fine, in fact.

I've worked hard on my parenting over the years. I've read books. I've intentionally used the knowledge I've learned from them. I've worked every day to improve my connection with my kids.

But I'm still far from a P.P.

If perfect parenting means I have the privilege of getting on a forum and pontificating on the virtues of P.P.s who raise perfect children, then I'm not interested.

Perfect Parent: Oh, come on. You know you want to be in our club.

Me: Thanks for asking, P.P. It's just that I'm washing my hair. Yes, every night this week. For all the evening hours. What's that? No, it's just that I have dirty hair, because my kids like to play with it. And, well, do you know how many nasty things live on kids' hands?

Perfect Parent: But don't you want a kid like mine? My kid

NEVER did THAT.

Me: Oh, I know what's going on, P.P. Your kid was so bad your memory blocked out the trauma of whole years. Well, I don't blame you. I don't remember the first year of having infant twins, and, frankly, I don't think I want to.

Here's the thing, though. Memories are often faulty. Looking back, we don't usually remember the hardest parts of parenting, the everyday stuff like tantrums over the blue plate instead of the orange one or the way he totally went all dramatic-crying on us when he stepped on a LEGO we've stepped on a million times and we had to stop the demonic laugh and the words it carried "YOU SEE? YOU SEE HOW IT FEELS?" We just remember the good stuff, the way he was such a good sleeper, the way he could stay buried in a book for hours at a time (but couldn't keep his attention on a math worksheet for two minutes). We remember those moments right before sleep, when he'd sneak back into our room (even though he was told not to) and give us "just one more kiss and hug."

We remember life much better than it actually was. This is a good thing. When I look back over my journals recording my first year with twins, they are filled with desperate cries for help. But what I actually remember from that time is a sweet little baby sleeping on my chest while I tried to quick-clean the living room because the dust on the shelves was an inch thick. What I remember is watching them sit in their Bumbo seats and the way they'd laugh because it was just like looking in a mirror. What I remember most is the way they would smile when any of their brothers came into view.

Perfect Parent: My memory's rock-solid, because, well, I'm perfect. My kid always did whatever he was told.

Me: Hey, I didn't know it was opposite day! Well, in that case, my kid always does whatever he's told, too.

Also, on the off-chance that you're not speaking in opposite-day language, that's a lot of absolutes, P.P. I don't like to speak in absolutes, personally. I do make an exception for this one, though: There is absolutely, positively no kid who does everything he's told. Absolutely. Positively. No way.

The easy kid who today will clean up all the Pattern Play blocks he got out at Quiet Time is the same kid who tomorrow will spend the whole of Quiet Time planning how he's going to run away because he doesn't want to clean up the LEGOs he dumped all over the floor. The kid who says this hour you're the best mom in the whole wide world because you let him color in his coloring book is the same kid who, two hours later, will call you the worst parent in the whole wide world because you said it wasn't time to turn flips off the couch while you're reading stories together. The kid who wants to do a puzzle with you right now is the same kid who, come bedtime, won't even want to kiss and hug you because he doesn't want to be anywhere near you and your mean self.

Parenting is full of paradoxes like these.

Here's the thing. There is no such thing as a perfect kid. There is no such thing as a perfect parent, either. The sooner we can wrap our heads around that, the better.

We're all just doing the best we can. I make mistakes. I do better. I love.

And today I made it through all the hours without thinking about putting them on Craigslist's free page.

At the end of the day, that's really all anyone can ask.

Why Do I Have to Be a Stay-at-Home Mom?

"Oh. You must be a stay-at-home mom."

There we sat, in a doctor's office for an annual exam, the nurse tapping in all my background information. We'd just established the six kids piece when she said it.

"No," I said. "Actually, I work full time."

It came out almost like an apology, like it usually does, like I know I should be ashamed to admit that I, a mother of six boys, work a full-time job, and I followed it up with a disclaimer about how I work from home in the afternoons and sometimes late at night so I can spend mornings and evenings with my children and actually do my work when they're being cared for by their daddy or they're asleep.

"Oh. Oh, wow," she said. "OK." She turned to put this latest bit of information into the computer with nothing more said.

It's not the first time I have encountered this assumption or felt the need to apologize for correcting it. It's usually women who make those comments, "So, obviously, you stay home with them all," "Wow, you must be way too busy to work a job," "Isn't it wonderful to stay home with them while they're little?" and it baffles me a little, because if there's one thing I've learned in my eight years of parenting, it's that we are all different.

Which means that what we think we might do if we had six children doesn't mean that's what another woman chooses to do.

There are moms of one child who choose to stay home with their child, and there are moms of six children who choose to work.

Every afternoon, I hole away in my home office and write essays and chapters of my latest book and a few poems in all the margins, and I thoroughly enjoy what I do. I always have. It's what I was made to do. Having children did not change that.

I work for myself, but I still choose to work. Because I am passionate about words and language and crafting beauty and truth to release out into the world. Because I believe in what I'm doing. Because I want my boys to know that women have as much to offer the world as they do.

But mostly because I am a better mother for my separate pursuit, for my writing, for the ways I can process through mistakes and circumstances and potential solutions outside of the constant demands of my children—but that is just me.

I have friends who are stay-at-home moms, and I love them dearly. I have friends who are working moms, and I love them dearly, too.

There is no one right way. There is only our right way.

We get really good at debating what's best for the children, but really what's best for the children is what's best for us. Some of us can be better versions of ourselves with a career to pursue. Some of us are better versions of ourselves away from the stress of an out-of-home job.

We can argue about who has it hardest, too, but it's all the hardest job in the world, because we are all mothers, and even when we're in an office, miles away from our children or just a few feet, we are still thinking of them and worrying about them and missing them. We are still loving them, just like any stay-at-home mom.

And when we're at home with them, meeting all those needs in real time, trying to hold fast to our sanity because all the whining is pulling it rapidly out of our reach, locking ourselves in the pantry for just a minute to breathe or think or eat that piece of chocolate we've been hiding, we are still thinking of them and worrying about them and loving them, just like any working mom.

Just because a mom chooses to mother six kids doesn't mean she chooses to stay at home full time or she has to give up on a career or she cannot pursue a dream for herself. It only means it may look different for her, like working odd hours to get all those tasks done, like trading off with their daddy to avoid childcare costs, like commuting to an office twice a week and working from a home office the other three days.

I don't work to get promotions or to make a lot of money or even to be some super-mom placed on a pedestal as a "she can do it, why can't I?" I work because it's enjoyable to me, because without writing and creating and chasing a dream, I am not the best version of myself.

I know that nurse didn't say those words to try to make me feel bad or guilty or wrong for my choice, and I don't. But I do believe that maybe the world could do without all our assumptions. Maybe the next time we see a mama with a whole tribe of kids crowding around her legs, fighting about who's going to ride her feet across the street this time, we don't just assume she is one who has chosen kids over a career, because it's the only way a thing like that would work.

Maybe we just admire those children, pat them on the head with an encouraging smile, and leave those assumptions where they lie.

Dear Concerned Reader: Yes, These Are All My Kids and Other Important Matters

After an essay of mine posted on a popular parenting site, people came out in droves to tell me why I should stop complaining and suck it up, grow up a little, or turn back time—because I probably should have never had kids. I collected all their comments and responded the best way I knew how. With humor.

"The hardest part of being a Mother is when they become adults and cut your heart to pieces."

"Wait until they're teenagers. Then you'll have something to complain about."

"Oh, please. Mothering isn't hard until they get to the teens."

-I Have it Worst

Dear I Have it Worst: I know I'm not a parent of a young adult yet. I know I don't have to figure out hormones and girlfriends and how to handle broken curfews. I know my little people are way easier to control than the big people they will one day be. But have you ever tried to wrestle a plunger that just went swimming in poo from four 3-year-old hands, and as soon as you finally peel those twenty fingers from the stick and turn around to put the (still-dripping) plunger somewhere they can't reach it, one of those four hands dips into the brown water to finish the job it wanted to do in the first place? Have you ever tried to stop an 8-year-old from digging out the old pacifiers from the trash can because he thinks they can be recycled into something new? Have you ever tried to convince a 5-year-old that horizontal stripes don't really match vertical stripes?

I know, I know. The answer is probably "I've done things much harder than that." I'm just trying to get you to practice this little amazing communication secret called "empathy," which means "to remember how it felt when your 3-year-old drew all over his brand new organic cotton sheets with a permanent marker you didn't know he had and you wanted to murder him." I bet you thought it was dang hard, too.

(This isn't a competition. Stop making it one.)

"A mother simply propagates a virus upon the earth. They all need to be destroyed."

—Violently Yours

Dear Violently Yours: Let's just use a little logic here. "A mother simply propagates a virus." For anything to propagate a virus upon the earth, that means it must have been a virus, too. I've been called a lot of things, but this one is new. A virus? That sounds intriguing. Like a mum flu or a mothebola virus. I sure wish that's what I were, because there are a lot of women in my life who would really like to have a baby. If I could infect them, you bet I would.

I know you meant your comment to be something far worse, but I feel like I have to thank you for the compliment. I'll remind you that a virus is **so small it can only be seen with a microscope.** Now. I've had six kids, including twins. There is no part of my body small enough to only be detected by a microscope. Maybe my brain. I can't seem to remember anything anymore. So I appreciate the vote of confidence in my ability to shrink back to regular (or nearly nonexistent) size after six children, but I assure you, we're not anywhere close.

Try again.

"I've met some really [bleep]-y mothers."

-What's Your Point

Dear What's Your Point: Welp, I'm not one of them. I actually rock at being a mother. The only thing I have in common with your comment is what I do most mornings at about 9 a.m., give or take a few.

"Sounds like whining to me and she has a husband to boot. I am a single mom and I don't feel this way. Thank God. There are some days when I want my son to leave me alone for 5 min but it's not hard. Suck it up butter cup!"

"SHUT THE HELL UP! You are a mother now grow up. She seems like a spoiled little brat who wants her single life with kids back again. Can't go back so look forward and be positive!"

-Parenting is Super Easy

Dear Parenting is Super Easy: I like this world you live in. How did you get there? May I please come, too? Because I live in a world where parenting is stinking hard, and it's not because I'm not a good mom or because I never should have had kids or because I want my single life back. It's just that I now live in a world where one of my kids will bust into my room in the middle of the night to tell me he feels like he needs to puke two seconds before he actually does, all over my comfy comforter that requires a bath in the tub and a stint out on the back porch to get clean. Now I have six boys who like to climb the walls like Spider-Man and put gigantic spitballs on the ceiling and leave LEGOs all over the floor so the baby is constantly in danger of choking on one of them. That doesn't mean I'd trade my life today for my no-kids one. IT JUST MEANS THAT IT'S HARD. It just means it's not perfect. It just means there are days I feel like tapping out, for a second or a minute or a whole afternoon.

Scratch that. I'm totally lying. The real reason it feels hard is because all I really want to do is lie on the couch and read the latest George R.R. Martin novel and sip on a little red wine so it dulls my senses and I don't have to hear the kids losing their minds about wanting dinner and why don't they ever have food and who's going to pour them milk. Why do kids have to be so dang hard?

"Are they all yours? My God."

-Tactless

Dear Tactless: What's a number you'd be comfortable with? One? Two? Maybe three? Well, then, that's how many are mine. The rest are strays who just thought we looked like better parents than the ones they had. And hey. What's a few more when you already have three?

What? They all look like me? Huh. That's weird. I guess I get around.

"You have enough for a basketball team. With a sub! Lolololololololol"

-Sports Analogies Are the Best

Dear Sports Analogies Are the Best: You smart thing. How did you guess? That's exactly what we were trying to do. We got married and, 18 months later, looked at each other and said, "WE SHOULD START A TOALSON BASKETBALL TEAM, because that would be really cool!" And now here we are. It's a really good thing we went for that sub, because a few of them can't dribble a ball without breaking their nose. I think we probably need a couple more, just to be safe.

"Are you done yet?"

-Just Call Me Nosy

Dear Just Call Me Nosy: Nope. We're not done until we beat the Duggars and get our own television show. Because that's the whole point of having babies, isn't it? Breaking the record for how many babies a body can produce in twenty-five years and snagging your own reality show? I still have ten or fifteen good years of childbearing left, and you better believe we are going to use them.

"You were trying for a girl, weren't you."

-Big Mouth

Dear Big Mouth: No. I've wanted six boys since I was a little girl, and that's exactly what happened. Lucky me.

Also, what's wrong with boys? What's wrong with wanting more boys?

"Stop using your choice to have six kids as an excuse to do nothing else."

-Supermom

Dear Supermom: Gosh, I admire you. I'm sure you have a perfectly manicured yard and your homemade bread never caves in the middle and all your kids' shoes match and are on the right feet every morning. And your kids probably never turn in a school paper late. And you never yell when the 3-year-old sneaks out of bed and hoards all the toothbrushes in the blue cup for God knows what reason, even though he's been told and told and told not to wander and especially not to hoard toothbrushes because you're tired of buying toothbrushes. And you throw the most spectacular birthday parties on the block. I wish I could be you. I really do.

But, alas, the only thing I do all day is lie on the couch and watch my hoodlums tear up my house around me so I have a reason to blame them for everything. I can't clean house, because I have six kids. I can't cook dinner, because I have six kids. I've been wearing the same workout pants for four days, because I have six kids.

The gulf between you and me is light years apart, so I give. You keep being your awesome super mom self, and I'll keep being my despicable lazy mom self.

Thanks for commenting! If you have any personal issue with any of my answers, please email idontcare@babymakingfactory.com. And I'm sure I'll see you around again soon!

The Amazing Things I Do When One of My Kids is Sick

Disclaimer: This essay is, in no way, intended to make light of the serious illnesses that can beset children. It is unfair and awful and cruel to see children suffer, and we grieve with all the parents raising children who are seriously and gravely ill. May every child be healed of their chronic illnesses.

It's been a madhouse lately.

There's a birthday coming up, and there's Thanksgiving and Christmas and all the preparations that go along with birthdays and holidays, and then there's the massive amount of school papers falling at random on our countertop, drowning us, and the list of homemade Christmas gifts we're WAY behind on that keeps getting lost in all the shuffle.

Add to that twins and potty training and how they must be reminded every twenty minutes to keep their underwear dry and clean. And then on top of all that, add twins transitioning to big boy beds and how they must be put back in their beds forty billion times every night.

Like I said, it's a madhouse.

But then one of our twins got sick with a mysterious fever that only brought with it a headache and an uncontrollable urge to sleep it off. One 2-year-old down and I felt like I could conquer the world.

My boy slept all day, and the next day the virus hit his 4-year-old brother, and the twins felt incredibly easy without the extra dynamic of an older brother. And then it hit the other twin, and another 2-year-old slept all morning on the couch and gave his mama a break.

I don't always approach sickness with this thank-you embrace, because sometimes there's vomit (times six), and sometimes there's so.much.snot I could fill a factory order for glue, and sometimes there are sore throats and achy chests and rashes that can worry a mama sick. But this was just a low-grade fever, and we put cold compresses on their foreheads and thieves essential oil on the bottoms of their feet and then tucked them away in their beds, where they slept for half a day, got up only to drink some water and then slept the rest of the day, too.

It took one of them down at a time, and my household felt remotely manageable. It felt weird and eerie, too, but I wasn't about to begrudge myself the enjoyment of a much-needed, unexpected break.

The whole dynamic of a house can change when one boy is out of commission, curled up with a headache and a fever. By the time the virus finished with the fourth boy (it never hit the oldest), I felt like a superhero, because I had:

1. Cleaned out all the closets, eliminating the clutter I so desperately hate.

2. Rearranged our entire library—furniture and books (about five thousand of them—and that's not an exaggeration).

3. Rearranged my oldest son's room and closet.

4. Packed away unnecessary clothes.

5. Colored with a 5-year-old, who had to stay home from school one day.

6. Rocked the 4-year-old to sleep (never happens).

7. Held the 2-year-olds for half an hour at a time (never happens either).

8. Tidied the entire house without clothes and shoes and toys undoing all my hard work BECAUSE KIDS WERE SLEEPING!

9. Spoke in complete sentences when talking to Husband.

10. Slept. I went to bed without having to tell kids to be quiet and settle down fifteen thousand times. And it was AMAZING.

I wouldn't wish my children sick all the time (of course I wouldn't), but I would be lying if I said I didn't enjoy this recent break.

Today, the twins are flipping over the couch and the 4-year-old is walking on his hands through the living room and the 5-year-old is shrieking and spinning until he falls and the 8-year-old is turning up his Harry Potter audiobook loud enough so he can actually hear it over all the noise.

I sure am glad they're back, madness and all.

I'm Now Afraid to Let My Kids Roam. Wait. No I'm Not.

I keep reading all these stories about parents who are issued warnings from the powers that be for letting their kids walk home from the park by themselves, even though the oldest child is ten and the park is three blocks down the road. And parents taking hits because they let their kids play outside without constant supervision. And cops stepping in because, God forbid, a mom let her kid ride his bike down a road another "concerned" parent thought was too busy.

Every time I read another article about it and then (I know I shouldn't) scan the comments that look more like word vomit than intelligent conversation, I want to hold up my MYODB sign.

This sign stands for Mind Your Own Dang Business.

I also find, lately, that I always have this overwhelming urge to tell my mom thank you for letting me roam.

Not too long ago, my boys and Husband and I visited some of my childhood places, because I thought it would be fun for them (they complained the whole time—at least until I started telling slightly embellished stories, since my life obviously wasn't interesting enough as is). There was this one house we lived in on a pretty major road, across the street from some train tracks where we used to play on coal piles when I was a third-grader. A little more than half a mile down this road was an old gas station that sold bubble gum for ten cents.

My mom used to let my brother (10), my sister (6) and me (9) walk to that store, because we would pester her so effectively she would just yell, "Go!" at our backsides already racing out the door.

Do you know what we had to cross to get to the store? A HIGHWAY.

By ourselves.

All alone.

At 10, 9 and 6, in case you didn't catch that.

There was no crosswalk, no blinking lights, no stop sign. There was no adult standing in the middle of the street waving a fluorescent orange flag and blowing a whistle to stop traffic. There was only an open road, a 50 mph speed limit and three kids racing across when they judged it was safe.

Now. I know what we all say—that the world is a much different place than it used to be, and I hate that old, "I did it and I'm just fine" argument just as much as the next person, but really. Has the danger of crossing a highway changed all that much? It was, after all, the same highway where I remember watching my dog Chance spin in fifteen circles when a car slammed into him as we were all crossing to check the mail.

My mom taught us the dangers, and then she trusted us to navigate them.

We're not so great at trusting our kids anymore.

I know how it is. When I think of my oldest boy, who will be a third grader next year, walking his brothers (a first grader and a kindergartener) the three blocks home from school next year, I shake a little inside. What if he forgets to pick them up? What if he gets mad at them and leaves them behind? What if they forget to look both ways when they're crossing streets? They have to cross three of them, for God's sake, and what if the drivers are going too fast or staring at their phones instead of what's in front of them?

I can talk myself out of that freedom so easily. Because I love my children so much.

But I also love them enough to let them try.

If we never let our children try, how will they ever know the excitement of having this self-management responsibility? How will they ever experience those rites of passage that come with turning another year older? How will they learn to navigate the dangers in the world on their own?

Maybe I'm naïve about it, but I don't think the world at large has changed so much as the world of parenting has. My mother used to let us walk on a busy road without a shoulder or a sidewalk and cross a semi-busy highway because she knew all the other mothers who lived on the street. She knew they would watch out for her kids in the same way she would watch out for theirs when they rode their bikes down the same road on their way to the elementary school playground. To play—by themselves—on merry-go-rounds and unpadded seesaws and metal slides that scorched the backs of your legs when the sun was out and ripped off the tender skin if you were brave enough to go down it in shorts.

If we are so concerned for the safety of other people's children, maybe instead of calling the cops on a child's parents, because we don't agree with the way the child gets to roam in this dangerous world (There are predators! There are bullies! There are drivers! Predators, bullies and drivers, oh my!), we could just step in as an extra pair of eyes.

What this might look like is asking children, on their walk home, if they feel okay about walking alone. If they're feeling scared today. Whether they would like some company if they *are* feeling scared.

The other day, I was driving my two schoolboys home because it was raining, and along our way I saw a boy on the ground and another one punching him in the belly.

"Hang on," I told my boys, and I slammed on the brakes and jumped out of the car into the pouring down rain to investigate what looked like a pretty serious fight.

Turns out they were just two boys horsing around, and they carried on their walking way, probably laughing about another mom freaking out about nothing.

Do you know what didn't even cross my mind to do?

Call the cops on the parents who let them walk home by themselves.

That would have been ridiculous. Parents know their own kids, right? Maybe we should just LET THEM PARENT.

I don't want to be afraid to let my kids explore the world around them because some "concerned" person might make a call and Child Protective Services suddenly shows up at my door. I want to give them freedom to play and wonder and discover and, through it all, learn that they are capable of making their way in this scary, but mostly safe, world.

I'm tired of this culture of fear. We need to find our courage. We need to trust each other again.

Most of all, we need to mind our own dang business.

Now that I got that off my chest, it's time to send my boys out the back door and lock it.

A mama needs her break, after all.

An Open Letter to My Laundry: We're Finished, But Not Really. Ever.

Dear Laundry,

I know, I know. You think I haven't noticed how you've been waiting seven whole days in that smelly basket, spilling over onto the floor so little boys trample you on their way to bedrooms, how you're crumpled up in bathrooms and twisted across couches and even left in the cold car all night, how all you really want is someone to care.

I assure you, I've noticed. I wish I could say I'm sorry for not washing you sooner, like you wanted, but I'm not. Because I was playing, skipping through the city zoo and riding on a carousel, teaching my boys kickball on a big field of green, making little dolls out of clothespins and yarn and fabric, and it was beautiful and invigorating and fun.

I just can't say the same about you, Laundry.

Maybe I used to feel differently about you, back when Husband and I walked you to the laundromat and put you in three washers and sat holding hands while talking and writing songs and reading marriage books for the forty-five minutes it took you to wash, and then doing it again while we watched you tumble dry low for another forty-five. But you have gotten out of hand, Laundry. You have invaded where you were not wanted. You have rewarded my hours of care with next to nothing, trading scattered cotton smelling like feet for stacked cotton smelling like lavender and eucalyptus, and maybe I should be grateful for even that, but it's just not enough anymore, because, well, someone needs to put you away, and that honestly seems like it's asking a little too much. I don't have that much to give you, Laundry.

I'm sorry you stay draped across the back of our couch for days on end (or maybe it's weeks; I've lost count), only moving when little boys have run out of clean underwear and feel bothered enough about reusing their dirty drawers that they'll come rifling through your avalanche. And then you're not even neat stacks anymore. You're like a laundry volcano, waiting for someone to turn a flip off the couch and scatter you everywhere, which will happen in about two more seconds. I'm sorry I'm not so great at finishing you. But I'm not really. Sorry, I mean.

See, you're just a little too needy. I have a LOT of needy people in my house, and I don't really need more, but you, well. You must be done every single week, so many loads of you, or you start creeping into the places we don't want you—like the baby's bed (because twins have a fetish for clothes piles, especially when they're smelly) and the boys' bathroom (which has a floor I wouldn't even wish upon my worst enemy, except maybe) and, yes, even the refrigerator (we have a few absent-minded ones in the bunch. "Where'd my soccer socks go?" "You mean the dirty ones you wore yesterday and the day before that?" "..." "Did you try the refrigerator?" "Why the refrigera– Oh. Yeah, here they are. That's weird.").

I'm just...

I'm just tired of you.

You steal so much valuable time, Laundry. You're like a giant black hole, sucking those seconds and minutes and hours into an invisible time warp so I hardly know where my whole day has gone because of your intruding buzzer that, every half hour, screams, "Finish me."

Finish yourself, Laundry.

As if all that weren't enough, you're never, ever actually done. That last load spills out of the dryer, and there are still the clothes we're wearing today. Are you never satisfied? Is there never an end to your demands? Can I just be done for a second or three or fifty-million? You're like one of my kids, and I know people say that after three it's just "pull up another chair," but that's actually not true at all. It's more like "Just pull up another adult," because you suddenly realize that you're way out of your league. Or maybe it's more like "Just pull up another bottle," because who really wants to help the parents who chose to have six kids? A bottle of Merlot, that's who.

I need a break from you, Laundry. It's not me, it's you. I have more than enough people clinging to me. I have more than enough people stealing my time and space. I have more than enough people making a mess of things. I don't need another, even if it's just a pile of sweaty socks that smell like rotting skunks.

Besides, my little boys want to play cars, and I'm sorting you, dark and light and white and towels and blankets, eight loads a week. My little boys want to go on a nature walk, and I'm waiting for one-eighth of you to finish washing so I can put you in the dryer and start the next one-eighth of you before we leave. I just want to go to bed, and there you are, commandeering my sleeping space like an unwanted blanket.

You have some things to learn before we can move on, Laundry. Autonomy. Self-discipline. Moderation.

But I have a feeling you won't even make an effort. So, with a great long sigh (it's still going), I guess I'll have to say that though I would like to say it's finished, I know the truth of it. A mom's relationship with laundry is never finished. So I'll see you in our normal meeting place (all over the house) next Monday at 6 a.m. sharp. Don't be late. As if you ever are.

Your resigned partner,

Me

8 Low-Expectation Parenting Goals for the New Year

Every new year, Husband and I make goals for everything. And I mean everything. Spiritual goals, financial goals, personal goals, business-related goals, marriage goals, family goals, reading goals, learning goals. All kinds of goals.

We don't like resolutions, because resolutions are something you make and then break. We like goals, because goals are something we work toward and may or may not accomplish throughout the course of a year, but at least we know we tried—and just trying is to be applauded in the life of a parent.

I've been making goals since I was a kid. I know it's a little weird, but I was always that child. I wanted to finish my homework ten minutes faster and read twenty more books this year and eat black-eyed peas for New Year's lunch without gagging.

These days my goals are hardly more refined, mostly because I'm now a parent.

Here's a look at some of my parent-goals for the next year:

1. Get more sleep. Or nap more. Or pretend I've passed out for fifteen minutes on the couch. Anything to get kids to leave me alone.

I realize this is most likely more difficult than my idealistic little mind can even grasp, since we have a new baby coming in February and everyone knows new babies, added to five already-existing boys, equals no sleep. It may even equal negative sleep. But I have not given up on this goal that cycles back around every year, because someday. I just know someday.

2. Stop walking barefoot around the house.

I have this picture that went a little viral recently. It's a picture of my 8-year-old's room, where his 300,000 Lego pieces have multiplied all over the floor. And while Legos are supposed to remain contained in his corner of the house, they somehow migrate into all the other rooms, which means it's not even remotely safe to walk anywhere barefoot.

But why would I want to? My floors haven't been cleaned in WAY, WAY, WAY too long. I can't even stomach anymore what I may be stepping on.

Why are my socks sticking to the kitchen floor? You don't really want to know.

Everyone got slippers for Christmas this year, so that's what we'll all be wearing from here on out.

3. Clean the house at least once.

Hey, when you're the mom of five, going on six, boys, you have really, really, really low expectations. Boys undo all the hard work in seconds, just as soon as they remember they need to go to the bathroom. On that note…

4. Mark my bathroom as a "no boys allowed" space.

Lately we've been breaking up the boys for baths, bathing half of them in our nice garden tub and the other half in their own, smaller tub. My nice garden tub is now disgustingly dirty. I really don't know where all this dirt comes from. Their hair? Their faces? The bottoms of their feet? I can't even guess. Well, okay, I do have a theory: Dirt comes from Boy.

Not only have they destroyed my garden tub, but they use my toilet, the one toilet in the house I'd like to call mine. Sometimes they forget to pull the seat up (I realize this is the opposite of many of their male counterparts, but it's just one of the weird variations my boys have on habits of the male species), and since I'm usually the first one to sit on the toilet seat after it's been abused by a boy…well, let's just say I feel like crying when my derriere feels like it's taken a shower without the rest of me.

They are also, obviously, very proud of what comes out of their bodies into the toilet and so leave it there for all the world to see. Thanks for the unexpected present, boys.

Please, please, please, just give me a bathroom of my own.

5. Budget for a house cleaner.

I know this seems like the easy way out, but all the bathrooms in my house (including mine) smell like a whole pack of animals drowned in a sewer, and the glass surfaces (mirrors supposedly hung in kids-can't-reach places and a glass-top dining room table…what were we thinking???) are so smudged you can't even see your real face in them. Sometimes you'll wonder if your vision is going. Sometimes you'll be glad, because, well, if you don't notice the new wrinkles, they're not really there.

A house cleaner would be nice, I think, because I can't possibly keep up with all the hands and feet and elbows and knees and other parts that shouldn't be mentioned here.

6. Read fewer articles that lie to me.

These would be articles like those titled, "How to never have to clean your home" (about how people maintain on a daily basis so there's no deep cleaning that ever needs to be done) and "12 easy home projects to do in 15 minutes" (kids add three hours to that fifteen minutes) and "eating paleo can be affordable." These people have obviously never had children. Or five.

7. Go a whole day without whining or complaining. Invite my children to do the same.

Sometimes we get in these funks as parents, whining and complaining about what they're doing or not doing, and all the while they're watching us, and when we say, "Please talk in your big boy voice. I can't understand you when you're whining," do you know what they're thinking?

Same goes for you.

Yes, the same goes for us. So maybe one way to get our kids to stop whining and complaining is to stop doing it ourselves.

In my house, this might take some work.

8. Get better at asking for help.

I know our society encourages us to pretend like we've got everything perfectly handled. But we don't. Maybe we do about 5 percent of the time. Or 1 percent of the time. The other 95-99 percent of the time we're one dangerous thread away from snapping into crazy-parent mode, and we're wishing there was some kind of help and feeling mad at ourselves for not asking in the first place.

Asking for help isn't weakness. It's strength that isn't often celebrated.

I don't know how many of these goals will become a reality, but a mom can dream, right? And I'm dreaming big for the next year.

As if you couldn't tell.

Dear Concerned Reader: No, My Vag Doesn't Drag the Floor and Other Business Matters

I have a large family. Six children. In a world where people are choosing to have fewer children (or none at all), this can seem weird and crazy and, for some, unacceptable.

These people always come out to play when I mention anywhere in one of my essays or blogs that six kids live in my house.

I get it. Six kids is a lot. Many people can't imagine having that many, let alone *choosing* to have that many. It seems like a crazy, why-would-anyone-want-to-do-THAT kind of thing.

Their concerns range from whether these kids are all from the same dad (yes) all the way down to what my uterus looks like. So, since I don't plan to stop writing about my large family, I thought it would be fun to have a page of FAQs and FCs (Frequent Comments) where I could just send them to save time. Because I'm considerate like that and wouldn't want anyone to die wondering.

"You do know how they are conceived and (that) there are methods of preventing said conception, correct."

-I'm Real Original

Dear I'm Real Original: This is certainly the mystery of the century. And, to be honest, I really have no idea. You know how people joke about that woman whose husband just looks at her and she's pregnant? It's not a joke. That woman is me.

Please tell me how this happens. I really don't want any more of these…things…wrecking my home. So let's go get a cup of coffee and you can tell me the whole conception story. The more details, the better.

"I'd like to sit down with her and ask her exactly what she thinks she's giving society by having six kids. These people are so selfish it makes me sick."

-I Have No Kids

Dear I Have No Kids: Huh. That's weird. I didn't think I owed society anything.

(Also: My boys are awesome. I could care less what you think.)

"I think you have enough kids."

-The Child Police

Dear The Child Police: I'm glad you noticed. Thanks for not being afraid to tell me, because now I can finally stop procreating. Because I truly do care what you think, even if I don't care what I Have No Kids thinks. You are the police, after all.

"I prefer a dog. I've always wondered why someone would bring another awful human into the world."

-I Hate Everyone

Dear I Hate Everyone: I want to be offended by your words, but I just feel sad. I wish I could find you and let you know how important you are to the world. My guess is you didn't have anyone to tell you that as a kid. Growing up in a world like that stinks. But not everyone is an awful human (I'm not. Husband's not. My boys aren't, either.). I hope you find some not-awful humans soon.

"Children can be taught to take care of their things. A quiet home may be impossible, but it can be a controlled noisy."

"Do some parenting and much of that nonsense will stop."

"Manners and chores are taught, not everyone who has boys has a torn up home."

– Perfect Parent

There you are Perfect Parent! I'm so glad you could come around. I know you're super busy raising your perfect kids. Can you do us all a favor and start a parenting class for the rest of us dopes? We could learn so much from you. Just tell us where to sign up and I'll try to make sure I can't find a pen anywhere.

"It just sounds like they run free, without any constraints. If something were to happen to the mother, who would want to care for them?"

-I Don't Get Humor

Dear I Don't Get Humor: Your name says it all. We're speaking a completely different language.

"Take a step back and figure out routines to control their acting out behaviors."

-I Know Everything

Dear I Know Everything: That sounds way too hard. I'd rather just let them run wild and terrorize the world while I lie on the couch and dream about my life before children.

"Why on earth do parents saddle their kids with ridiculous names?"

"What a bunch of bizarre names you've selected for your boys, lady."

-Names Are My Business

Dear Names Are My Business: I didn't realize I was in violation of the "Acceptable Names According to Society" list. Next opportunity I have, I'll march on down to the courthouse and change their names to something that might be easier for you to stomach.

Or maybe I'll just take a shower. Because it's been a while, and opportunities are opportunities.

Shower or courthouse? Shower or courthouse? Shower or courthouse?

Aw, dang. Shower won.

Welp. Guess you'll have to get used to those ridiculously bizarre names.

"What were you drinking when you named them?"

-I Know Names

Dear I Know Names: That would be peppermint Schnapps, straight from the bottle. Because, you know, they allow that at the hospital during a woman's childbirth recovery period. By the time the birth certificate official came around I couldn't feel my tongue anymore. You know what happens next.

Let that be a lesson, people. Don't drink while naming children.

"If they are anything like the Duggars..."

"Is she related to the Duggars or just another dimwit breeding for the heck of it?"

"Trying to be like the Duggars or something?"

-I Can't Count

Dear I Can't Count: I know, I know. Six is so close to nineteen. Scarily close. Turn around, and I might have more children than the Duggars tomorrow.

Truth be told, we're trying to be like another famous family. Just call us the Weasleys.

"What I learned from six boys: have a vasectomy."

"Should've had an abortion at some point."

-No Tact

Dear No Tact: What an educated, insightful answer. I'm so glad you could contribute something valuable to this discussion.

"Maybe booze has something to do with you guys getting pregnant so many times?"

-Stay Away From Alcohol

Dear Stay Away From Alcohol: I don't really remember. All I know is every day I had to buy a new bottle of red wine from the corner store because the old one just kept mysteriously disappearing.

"She should have told her husband to put that thing away after birth #3."

-Sexpert

Dear Sexpert: I did. Didn't work. Mostly because I look dang good in yoga pants and an unwashed-hair ponytail.

"She is discusting." (stet)

-Phonics is Hard

Dear Phonics is Hard: Sorry, I don't take insults from people who can't spell. Maybe that's snobbish. But I'm just being honest. Come back to visit once you learn how to spell the word "disgusting."

"They sound like the worst parents ever."

-I Share Opinions

Dear I Share Opinions: We *are* the worst parents ever. Just ask any of our kids when they have immediate lights out for getting out of bed for the third time and someone's not dying (which constitutes an emergency). Just ask them when they get an extra chore for leaving the table without being excused. Just ask them when they aren't allowed to watch the new *Diary of a Wimpy Kid* movie like all their friends do because the content is too mature.

"No wonder there's not a husband in the picture. She's ugly."

-Fugly and Fffffpppsmart

Dear Fugly and Fffffpppsmart: I know it's really hard to understand, but there is this thing that happens when someone takes a picture. It's called Standing Behind the Camera. You see, someone has to stand *behind* the camera in order for a picture to be taken (unless you set an auto-picture, which I have no idea how to do. Technology's not my strong point. Having babies is.). Husband was behind the camera.

Please don't let your brain explode with this amazing revelation.

"I know your hands are full, but you chose to have a large family, and it is time for you both to step up and be responsible. Do them a huge favor and try to have them become gentlemen. Make them pick up their own clothes instead of leaving them all over the floor. The world will thank you."

-Concerned Non-parent

Dear Concerned Non-parent: Well, this just dashes all my parent-hopes. I guess I thought my boys would leave their clothes on the floor forever, or at least until they found a wife to pick up after them. I definitely didn't plan on teaching them to find the hamper or clean up their own messes or do their own laundry. Mostly because I LOVE BEING A MAID.

(Said no mother ever.)

"Her uterus must be dragging the floor just like her vag."

-Crude Dude

Dear Crude Dude: Kind of you to be concerned. As far as I

know, I haven't tripped over either yet, so I think I'm doing okay.

"Women like this keep popping out kids to try and remain relevant because they have no skills or talent. Get an education, lady...they will teach you how to keep ur legs closed."

-School Fixes Everything

Dear School Fixes Everything: I must be dumber than I thought. What does "ur" mean? I've never come across that word in my study of the English language.

Oh, wait. Study? I've never done that. It probably wouldn't surprise you to know that I did not graduate valedictorian of my high school class, and I didn't get a full ride to a university of my choice, and I most definitely didn't graduate four years later with a 4.0 GPA and a degree in print journalism and English. Because, you know, women like that don't have trouble keeping their legs closed. They know where babies come from, and they make sure they don't have six of them.

I'm sure it also wouldn't surprise you to know that I've never, ever, in all my life, won a writing award or been recognized for any of my work, because, of course, I have zero talents.

Now I feel sad that I didn't do more with my life. Guess I'll go open that new bottle of red wine and have another baby.

Thanks for commenting! If you have any personal issues with any of my answers, please email idontcare@babymakingfactory.com.

See you next time I write an article about my big family!

The End

Don't miss out on a Crash Test Parents release! Visit www.crashtestparents.com to keep up-to-date on book and product releases and to access bonus material.

Appendix A: 20 Confessions of a Real Parent

1. When your kid says, "I'm bored," and you want to say, "Trade me places for an afternoon. I would love to be bored. Why do you get to have all the fun?"

2. When your kid dropkicks his instigating brother and you want to say, "Let that be a lesson in natural consequences."

3. When your kid says, "He's looking at me," and you want to turn to the driver in the car next to you and say, "Stop looking at me," just to prove a point. And you do. And quickly realize the person next to you is your son's elementary school principal.

4. When your kid asks if he can have a snack after eating five pounds of grapes and you want to joker-laugh in his face.

5. When your kid sneak-eats a whole bag of apples and you want to say, "When you crap your pants, don't come running to me."

6. When your twins start singing "I came in like a wrecking ball," and all you can do is think, *Yep. You sure did.*

7. When your kid sings the ABCs on repeat and you start singing the Pokémon theme song just to get something else in his

head.

8. When your kid says "Are you pregnant again?" and you want to say, "Exaggerate much? I just had a piece of chocolate."

9. When your kids (FINALLY!) go outside to play and you want to lock them out for the rest of the evening.

10. When your kid says he wants to dig a hole in your front yard, and you want to say, "What, so I can bury you in it?"

11. When your kid starts talking about Minecraft and you start looking for the fast-forward button.

12. When your kid gets out of bed for the thousandth time tonight and you start thinking a "mental health" bed would be a viable option for restraint.

13. When your kid says he can't find his shoes that are right in front of his face and you want to pick them up, juggle them, and say, "Can you see them now?"

14. When your 4-year-old pees off the side of the deck onto the brand new ($6,000) air conditioner unit and you want to rearrange his "What did I do?" face.

15. When your kid says his friends don't do chores and you're the worst parent ever and you want to do a victory dance in your

kitchen because this is your first parenting award.

16. When your kid says stop talking to him because you have bad breath and you want to say, “Well, I guarantee it isn’t as bad as what came out of your bunghole once upon a time.”

17. When your kid leaves stray toys out, because cleaning up is no fun, and you want to toss them all and go 19th century childhood on him.

18. When your 5-year-old old says can he PLEASE vacuum and you want to squeal as much as he does when you say yes. But you don't want to seem too eager.

19. When someone gives your kid shoes with laces and he can’t tie his shoes yet. And you’re running late. And they’re the only shoes he wants to wear. And you want to die.

20. When your kids won’t stop arguing and you want to join in on the slap fight that breaks out amongst them.

Appendix B: 10 Helpful Pro Tips Gleaned From the Lives of Kids

How to clean your room:

1. Pile everything on your brother's bed.
2. Get "too tired."
3. Shove it all on the floor when it's time for bed.
4. Do it all again tomorrow.

How to blow up a balloon:

1. Refuse the help of your mom.
2. Put the open part in your mouth.
3. Spit.
4. Hand it back to your mom soaking wet and ask her to blow it up now.

How to clean a house:

1. Walk around in circles.
2. Complain.
3. Pick up one thing.
4. Complain.
5. Repeat until your mom sends you outside.

How to get a parent's attention:

1. Scrunch up your voice so it resembles a scream-whine.

2. Say their name.
3. Repeat as many times as it takes.

How to play the guessing game:

1. Say, "Guess what?"
2. Actually wait until they guess.
3. Seriously, they have to guess.
4. Never tell.

How to smell like a locker room:

1. Be a boy.
2. Forget you should be wearing deodorant.
3. Repeat.

How to leave the house on time:

1. Say you can't find your shoes.
2. Run around madly looking for them.
3. Find them.
4. Run screeching out the door.
5. Make sure you run screeching out the door.

How to clean up your toys:

1. Toss them in the air.
2. Spin in circles as they fall around you.
3. Lie down.
4. Say you're too tired.
5. Act shocked when you mom takes them away.

How to jump off a trampoline:

1. Make sure your brother is on the ground where you'll land.
2. Yeah, that's really all.

How to win a fight:

1. Hit your brother first.
2. Run.

About the Author

Rachel is the CCO (Chief Complaints Officer) in her rowdy and wild home, working most hours between dinner time—because she and Husband are the only parents in the world who make their children do chores, according to their children—and bedtime—because bedtime is synonymous with let's-see-how-often-we-can-get-out-of-our-beds-before-Mama-and-Daddy-explode time.

She can frequently be seen wrestling permanent markers out of her toddler twins' hands, doing Matrix moves to avoid her baby's sticky fingers, and standing in as The Best Place to Sit when she and her boys read stories—which is, collectively, more than an hour every day.

When she's not doing any of these things, Rachel is holed up in her bedroom, running a writing business and cranking out 5,000 words a day five days a week. Her essays have been published on Huff Post, Babble, Scary Mommy and other publications across the world. She lives in San Antonio, Texas, with her husband and six boys.

Author's Note

My dear reader,

There is absolutely nothing in the world like being a parent. It's beautiful, it's hard, it's wonderful, it's hard, it's fun, it's hard. I've done a lot of challenging things in my life, and parenting is one of the hardest. But also one of the most significant. One of the most beautiful.

I write my personal essays and open a window into the life of my family, because in the span of a day, there are a billion things that can and do, often, go wrong. I get a little bent out of shape when they do. But writing humorous essays about these happenings has loosened me up a little. I sincerely hope that reading them has also loosened you up a little—because the only way to live life when you're raising little irrational human beings is with a liberal dose of humor.

Thank you for supporting my work. Please consider leaving a review wherever you bought it. Reviews help do a number of things—most notably get the book into the hands of other parents who are at their wits' end.

Thank you for reading.

In love,
Rachel

Acknowledgements

This book would not have been possible without my amazing husband, who is also my graphic designer, my video guy, my branding consultant and my first reader. Thank you for being you and for loving me.

And, of course, the pages of this book would have sat empty if not for my six marvelous, maddening, beautiful boys. J, A, H, Z, B, Ash, I love you immensely. If all the seas on the planet Earth joined together as a measure of my love, I would need billions more.

And to all my blog readers, who made a book feel necessary. Thank you for reading and sharing and laughing right along with me.

www.ingramcontent.com/pod-product-compliance
Lightning Source LLC
Chambersburg PA
CBHW021430080526
44588CB00009B/485
* 9 7 8 1 9 4 6 1 9 3 1 5 5 *